SMITHSONIAN INSTITUTION
BUREAU OF AMERICAN ETHNOLOGY
BULLETIN 141

CERAMIC STRATIGRAPHY AT CERRO DE LAS MESAS VERACRUZ, MEXICO

By

PHILIP DRUCKER

I0123312

UNITED STATES
GOVERNMENT PRINTING OFFICE
WASHINGTON : 1943

LETTER OF TRANSMITTAL

SMITHSONIAN INSTITUTION,
BUREAU OF AMERICAN ETHNOLOGY,
Washington, D. C., November 16, 1942.

SIR: I have the honor to transmit herewith a manuscript entitled "Ceramic Stratigraphy at Cerro de las Mesas, Veracruz, Mexico," by Philip Drucker, and to recommend that it be published as a bulletin of the Bureau of American Ethnology.

Very respectfully yours,

M. W. STIRLING, *Chief.*

Dr. C. G. ABBOT,
Secretary of the Smithsonian Institution.

CONTENTS

ILLUSTRATIONS

PLATES

(All plates at end of book)

1. (Frontispiece.) Cerro de las Mesas Polychrome wares. Dull Buff Polychrome, Brown Polychrome, Black-and-White-on-Red, and Complicated Polychrome.
2. Complicated Polychrome sherds: Jar exteriors, bowl interior.
3. Brown Polychrome bowl sherds.
4. Trade wares.
5. Trade wares.
6. Trench 30. Objects associated with burial II–18.
7. Trenches 31 and 33. *a*, Stucco floor, trench 31; *b*, buried stairway, trench 33.
8. Monumental ware from trenches 7 and 34.
9. Views of jade cache, trench 34.
10. Trenches 34, 13, 14–A, and 15. *a*, View of jade cache from trench 34; *b*, trench 13; *c*, remnants of "pipe line," trench 14–A; *d*, Plumbate vessel in intrusive pit, trench 15.
11. Trench 40. *a, b*, Ollas containing skulls; *b* shows relation to stucco layers.
12. Trench 42.
13. Burials I–1 to I–6 (*a-f*).
14. Burials I–7 to I–10 (*a-d*), I–14 (*e*), and I–16 (*f*).
15. Brown ware vessels.
16. Brown ware vessels
17. Brown ware ollas.
18. Polished Brown ware.
19. Black ware vessels.
20. Black ware vessels.
21. Stucco Painted ware from burial II–18.
22. Miscellaneous wares.
23. Plumbate whistling jar from trench 15.
24. Bottles in form of Tlalocs. Purchase collection.
25. Plain ware ollas and jars.
26. Wares and figurine molds.
27. Hand-made punctate figurines (Type I).
28. Miscellaneous type I figurines: variants, animal forms, etc.
29. Type II–A figurine heads.
30. Type II figurines with flat bodies.
31. Type II–A figurines with flat bodies.
32. Type II figurines with hollow bodies.
33. Type II–B figurines, representing dead persons or Xipe.
34. Type II figurines, representing Tlalocs and Death's Heads.
35. Type II figurines: variant headdresses; monkeys.
36. Type II figurines, representing animals.
37. Variant type II figurines.

TEXT FIGURES

CERAMIC STRATIGRAPHY AT CERRO DE LAS MESAS, VERACRUZ, MEXICO

By Philip Drucker

INTRODUCTION

The present report is a study of the ceramics recovered by the National Geographic–Smithsonian Institution Expedition at the site of Cerro de las Mesas, Veracruz, Mexico, in 1941. Mr. Stirling, the expedition leader, has reported on the season's work, and described the important finds of other materials (Stirling, 1941), and therefore this account will be restricted to a consideration of the pottery and the chronological sequences represented by the expedition's collection of this material. Such a division conforms to the program of the investigations, as mapped out by the leader of the expedition. The tasks of clearing and studying the stone monuments and of excavating the mounds and other structures were under the direct charge of Stirling; the stratigraphic excavations in the refuse deposits were entrusted to the writer.

In plan, this account will parallel that of the 1940 excavations at Tres Zapotes, to which it is similar in both subject and aim. For the sake of orientation, the site geography will be described, and followed by an account of the excavations. A third section will establish the typology of the Cerro de las Mesas wares, and a fourth will present their vertical distributions in the stratitrenches, and will define the divisions represented in the ceramic column. In a final chapter, an attempt will be made to place the Cerro de las Mesas ceramic column chronologically by means of internal and comparative evidence.

THE LOCAL GEOGRAPHY

The site of Cerro de las Mesas is situated in southern Veracruz in the low-lying plain bordering the Bay of Alvarado on the west (fig. 1). It lies between the Río Blanco on the north and another stream (for which we were unable to learn any other name than "el río") a mile and a half to the south. The latter is a tributary of the Blanco, joining it not far from the bay.

1

The prevailing local land-form is that of the "potreros" or "cienegas," to use the local terms, low areas that flood in the wet season,[1] forming nearly impassable and completely uninhabitable swamps. The remainder of the year they dry out, providing rich pasture lands for the modern inhabitants. The entire structure is built-up swamp that once flanked a wider bay. Here and there are elevated areas, for the most part sandy, rising islandlike (in the wet season this is not a simile, but a reality) above the plain. These formations vary in area from several acres to several square miles. None attain notable height; for the most part they rise gradually, almost imperceptibly, from the potreros to a maximum elevation of 15 or 20 feet. Their borders are marked not by cut banks or sharp declivities, but by noticeable changes in soil type and vegetation. The soil of the low areas is black, heavy, and clayey, with a marked tendency to cracking in dry weather. Unfortunately, the writer was not able to identify the typical potrero floral assemblage properly; the two most conspicuous members are a tall, very coarse grass known locally as "camalote," and a thorny bush with small compound leaves called "zarza." It is worth noting that in the course of extensive reconnaissance in the environs of the site not a trace of aboriginal occupancy was found in the potreros.

The Cerro de las Mesas site occupies one of the larger of the sandy "islands." In point of fact, it is probably more correct to say that Cerro de las Mesas is one of a series of sites distributed along the crest of an "island" 10 or 12 miles long by 2 or 3 miles wide, extending from the modern village of Cocuite to Ignacio de la Llave. These sites appear as concentrations of earth mounds with their accompanying occupational deposits. The latter are not particularly conspicuous. If size and number of mounds and the occurrence of stone monuments are any indication, the Cerro de las Mesas group was probably the populational and ceremonial center of the region.

For descriptive purposes, the site may be divided into a number of localities. The first and most striking is the Central Mound Group, consisting of several closely set high mounds and platform mounds situated so as to form a number of enclosures or "plazas." (See fig. 1.) The tallest of the high mounds, that from which the site takes its name, attains a height of 50 to 60 feet, and is about 200 feet square at the base. The platform mounds are quite sizable structures, several hundred feet across. Their height is difficult to estimate, the more so since natural elevations may have been utilized as bases for them, but 10 to 20 feet seems about right. It should be mentioned that it is here, in the Central Mound Group, that the stone monuments occur.

---

[1] The climate is of the "Tropical" type, with a single wet season, from June to December, and a dry season, January to May.

A quarter mile to the southwest, in and just beyond the modern village of Paso del Bote, are the outliers of another group of large mounds. These, however, are less compactly grouped than those just described; in fact, it is difficult to say if they really formed an integrated arrangement, or are independent units. In between them, and around the Central Group, are numerous small mounds, for the most part situated without apparent relation to each other or to the major features, which obscure any original systematic arrangement. To the north-northeast of the Central Group, as well, are other large mounds.

North of the Central Group, and extending some distance to the west, is an open nearly level plain, on which there are but few mounds. This is the locality which proved to be the principal occupation zone of the site. It was here that the deepest and most extensive refuse deposits were found. At its western end, about a mile from the Central Group, the deposit underlies a hodgepodge of small mounds, which form the northwestern end of the site and which we may distinguish as the Small Mound Locality. These mounds range from 8 to 15 feet in height, and from 30 to 100 feet across. There are no apparent arrangements of plazas, or the like. It may be noted that these structures, like those interspersed among the large mounds, are not house mounds, in the sense of foundations for dwellings. All those investigated revealed features indicative of ceremonial functions.

These localities complete the list of those in which explorations of importance were made in the 1941 season. To the south and east of the Central Group are numerous small mounds, with here and there a structure or group of structures of moderate size. Since however, none of these were excavated, and since intensive search disclosed no occupational deposits of consequence, these portions of the site need not be described in any detail.

There remains to be considered the relationship of the site, mounds, and habitational localities to water supply. "The river," as local people refer to it, is the nearest present-day stream. It lies a good mile and a half from the southern edge of the site. The Río Blanco passes several miles to the north. In short, there is no close running water, at least in the dry season. Modern inhabitants depend upon wells that tap the shallow water table. Along the northwestern end of the site, however, runs an old partially filled stream bed. Half or three-quarters of a mile west of the Central Mound Group, the bed angles southeastward cutting through the site. It is probable that during at least a part of the site's history this channel bore the water of "the river" within more convenient distance, and that not until later times did the flow break through to the lower potreros to the south where it now runs. After the epochs of construction, borrow pits provided watering places in the wet season. A large one, at the south end of the Central Mound Group, is said to contain water all through the dry season in normal years. (It was full in February of 1940, when Stirling first inspected the site. In 1941 it was dry, presumably because of the unusual dryness of the year 1940.) Other smaller pits are to be found here and there on the site, and are particularly numerous in the Small Mound Locality in the northwest. However, the excavations in the occupational zone give evidence that in the earliest periods the topography of the site differed somewhat, and that probably springs and trickles of water, if not streams, were close at hand.

THE DEPOSITS

To complete the picture of the site, it is necessary to discuss the nature of the formations in which and on which cultural remains occur. The matrix of materials recovered from mound excavations, being secondary or redeposited mix apparently of the same nature as the primary deposit, needs no special consideration. Reference, therefore, is to the primary refuse deposits in the open plain to the north and northwest of the Central Mound Group.

The basic structures of the site have been referred to briefly. The "island" on which it is situated is composed principally of light sandy soil. Although the present surface in the occupational locality is nearly level, it was not always so. The sandy soil, or rather soils, occur in layers which vary in thickness and inclination. A section through the complete series indicates clearly that we have to do with wind-deposited formations, dunes, in short, which became anchored down, and eventually leveled off. The cultural remains occur in the uppermost of these sand layers, superimposed on the irregular rolling surface of the old dunes. The human occupancy of the site thus began at a time when the locality had begun to assume its present elevated character, and continued through the period of reworking and leveling off of the dunes. The sandy soils lie upon a nearly level horizon of finely divided very heavy soil, dark purplish brown in color, apparently an old swamp muck, completely sterile of cultural debris wherever tested, although in the hollows between the dunes the culture-bearing strata lie directly on this subsoil.

It is worth mentioning that the sandy soils of the deposits and dunes differ in an important respect from the more common tropical clay soils in that they are very strongly basic. Not only is this immediately noticeable in the local well water, but numerous concretions, apparently of a calcium carbonate, occur in the soils, and osseous materials are heavily permeated with the same material. In fact, in many cases the marrow canals of bones are filled with crystals. The source of this material is not of immediate concern, though it may be pointed out that if the sands are beach sands from the bay, they well may have contained ground-up particles of shell and other calcium-rich substances. More important is the fact that this soil condition makes possible the recovery of skeletal material, and, as well, sherds, particularly of painted wares, are much better preserved than those embedded in the more common acid clays.

The cultural remnants found in these deposits consist primarily of potsherds, with odds and ends of other materials; fragments of manos and metates, prismatic flakes of obsidian, now and then a bit of worked bone, an awl or similar object, and a fair amount of animal bone, probably kitchen refuse. Charcoal and ash occur in varying quantities. For the most part, the trenches sectioned what appeared to be dumps, rather than actual midden areas, but a few instances of floors and fire pits were found. In additition to this primary refuse, a few instances of inclusions of other types were found; cache lots of vessels, and burials. Unlike the mounds, however, the primary deposits yielded but few cache lots, and those of vessels of very ordinary types, and the burials were rarely accompanied by offerings.

THE EXCAVATIONS

In the course of the 1941 season, 36 trenches, numbered as in table 1, were dug at Cerro de las Mesas. In this series are included investigations of structures, test pits, and stratigraphic sections. Table 1 shows the type and location, in terms of the several localities just described, of each trench. (See also site map, fig. 1.)

All the excavations in the Central Mound Group except trench 1 were dug by Stirling. The rest of the trenches were dug by the writer.

In addition to the formal trenches, a number of prospect pits were dug at various points on the site, in an attempt to find culture-bearing deposits. Various localities in and adjacent to the mound groups were shown to be sterile for all practical purposes, even though in some places a few sherds occurred in the uppermost soil layers. Such localities are marked "S" on the map. The test trenches and prospects indicate that the main occupation area or areas of the site lie along its northern and northwestern edge. Here, and here only, were primary refuse deposits found which had more than a few scant inches of depth. It is not impossible that other primary deposits occur at Cerro de las Mesas, but if so they are well buried, and can be found only by chance.

The trench descriptions will follow the order of the tabulation given on page 6,[2] beginning with those of the Central Mound Group.

---

[2] Except for trench 1, described at the end of this section.

Table 1.—*Type and location of 36 trenches dug at Cerro de las Mesas*

Trench No.	Type	Locality
1	Test pit	Central Mound Group.
7	Structural section	Do.
12	----do----	Do.
15	----do----	Do.
16	----do----	Do.
30	----do----	Do.
31	----do----	Do.
32	----do----	Do.
33	----do----	Do.
34	----do----	Do.
2	Test pit	Occupational area.
4	----do----	Do.
10	----do----	Do.
11	Stratitest (incomplete)	Do.
13	Stratitest	Do.
17	Test pit	Do.
18	----do----	Do.
20	----do----	Do.
21	----do----	Do.
22	----do----	Do.
23	----do----	Do.
24	----do----	Do.
25	----do----	Do.
26	----do----	Do.
3	----do----	Do.
5	----do----	Do.
27	----do----	Do.
28	----do----	Do.
14	Structural section	Small Mound Locality.
19	----do----	Do.
40	----do----	Do.
41	----do----	Do.
42	Stratitest	Do.
6	Structural section	Western Mound Group.
8	Test pit	Southern edge of site.
9	----do----	Do.

Since the tests and stratitrenches were dug for the most part in groups or systems, they are described in groups rather than according to numerical sequences (the field excavation numbers were retained despite irregularities of order, etc., to avoid the danger of mixing field-numbered specimens).

The mound and structural investigations were put down without regard to levels, either natural or arbitrary. The aim of these excavations was to recover information as to the aboriginal constructions, and to assemble ceramic data particularly in the form of cache associations. Both goals were amply fulfilled. Indeed, our knowledge of Cerro de las Mesas ceramics would be woefully incomplete were it not for the mound material, for not only were there recovered many complete and restorable vessels whose forms could not have been reconstructed from the test and stratitrench fragments, but certain wares, presumably ceremonial varieties, were found only in the mounds.

Trench 7 was, properly speaking, a system of trenches dug in the elevated intermound plaza, in an attempt to find stelae, or stone monuments, reported there. Two stones were found, one on the south and one on the west side of the plaza. Stirling has described these elsewhere (Stirling, 1941). Near each of the stones were found fragmentary portions of the large ornate Stucco-Painted "incensarios" and a few human-bone fragments. One of the incensarios was apparently in the form of a Tlaloc (or with an attached mask representing that deity), coated with white stucco paint. Beneath it was a red-painted base or stand, and various fragments of large figurines.

Trench 12 was the number assigned to the excavations made in the course of clearing and setting up the various stone monuments in the "Monument Plaza."

Trench 15 was dug for the purpose of clearing a structure (or foundation of a structure) in the eastern portion of the Monument Plaza. This proved to be a rectangular enclosure, faced on the exterior and upper edge with layers of painted "stucco" or lime made of calcined shells and sand. The eastern edge lay directly against the base of a large mound to which the whole feature probably belonged. In fact, it centered very well on the sets of stairs uncovered in the trench put through this mound (trench 34), to be described. In plan, the structure consisted of two conjoined rectangles (without an intervening wall). The eastern rectangle was slightly wider and higher than the western one. The measurements were: Length (east-west) 33 feet; width west end 34 feet, east end 34 feet; height west end 3 feet 4 inches, east end 3 feet. A set of steps led up the front (west) edge of the platform. It should be noted that several of the stone monuments occurred on and close to the platform or foundation, without obvious relation to it. (See Stirling, 1941, p. 284.) Presumably they were put there after the feature had been buried by slope-wash from the surrounding mounds, or, conceivably, by artificial filling in.

A number of burials, all in a rather poor state of preservation, were encountered in the course of clearing the feature. While those within the area of the stuccoed walls are difficult to relate temporally to the structure, those found just outside were obviously interred subsequent to its covering, for all lay at a depth less than that of the base of the wall.

Within the area, at the midpoint of the east wall, were two secondary child burials. By the skull of one of them were two jade beads. Directly across the compound, just outside the west wall, were the remains of six individuals, all children, in a pit 26 inches deep marked clearly as intrusive by the black (humus-stained) pitfall. These burials also appeared to be secondary inhumations. Three were placed with the skulls touching. With the remains were a considerable number of jade beads, mostly close to the skulls. In the bottom of the pit, upside down, was a Plumbate whistling jar, in the form of an individual holding a spouted teapotlike vessel on his lap (pls. 10, d; 23). The vessel was absolutely intact (until "found" by a workman's pick), with a sheen that gives it a very new and unused appearance.

Trench 16 was a cut made to clear a stone monument situated a short distance away from the rest. The excavation disclosed a low earth platform, 6 feet square and 13 inches high, with rounded corners. (Stirling, 1941, p. 282.) It was faced with several layers of stucco, the outermost of which had red-painted corners.

Trench 30 was staked off 36 feet east-west by 15 feet north-south from the western edge through the center of a small flat-topped mound on the northwest corner of the large platform mound of the Central Group. Stirling has described this section in some detail in his report (Stirling, 1941, pp. 282–287); it will be necessary only to summarize his account and tabulate the principal finds, consisting of burials with accompanying artifacts.

The mound consisted of two parts: a low primary structure 30 inches high above the platform mound, and extending 27 feet out from the head (east) end of the trench; and a covering or enlargement which attained a maximum height of 66 inches above the primary mound (fig. 2). The latter was constructed principally of a buff clayey soil which contrasted with the grayish-brown mix of the covering. The

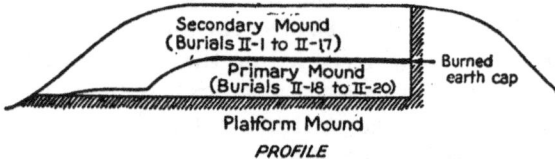

Secondary Mound
(Burials II-1 to II-17)
Primary Mound
(Burials II-18 to II-20)
Burned earth cap
Platform Mound
PROFILE

FIGURE 2.—Trench 30, profile, north wall.

contact of the two layers was emphasized by the layer of burned earth that capped the inferior structure.

A total of 20 burials were recovered from this excavation, 17 of which were in the upper level, 3 in the low primary mound. The principal features of the interments are shown in table 2. It should be mentioned that burials in the mounds were consistently in a poorer state of preservation than those of the refuse deposits of the Occupational Locality.

One hardly knows how to classify the four finds (II–12, II–14, II–16, and II–17) consisting of only facial portions of skulls. They might represent interments, perhaps of victims of sacrifice, or they might be trophies. At any rate, the occurrence of four such specimens, neatly stowed away in pottery containers, points to an established pattern. Among the features of the remaining burials from the upper layer of the mound, we may note particularly the occurrence of the custom of placing a shell on or near the face, suggesting a definite connection with the burials from the Occupational Locality to be described. To be noted, too, is the fact that the burials with few or no other grave offerings were accompanied by the drab fresh-water shells, whereas the more richly equipped remains often (though not invariably) had marine shells associated with them.

As to the time interval separating the two sets of burials, those of the upper and of the lower mound strata, little can be said as yet.

TABLE 2.—*Principal features of burials found in trench 30*

Burial No.[1]	Position	Associations	Remarks
II-1	Semiflexed	None	
II-2	----do----	----do----	
II-3	----do----	----do----	
II-4	----do----	River clamshell near mouth	
II-5		Red-painted marine shell near head; 7 pottery vessels;[2] 1 figurine; 5 marine shells; 1 jade bead; 1 perforated canine tooth.	
II-6		River clamshell over mouth	
II-7		1 large pottery vessel	Face covered with lime and red paint.
II-8		2 jade ear plugs; 10 jade beads; 10 beads of black substance (wood?); 1 carved jade ornament; 1 canine tooth.	Bones covered with red paint.
II-9		1 pottery vessel (possibly belongs to II-8?).	
II-10		1 miniature pottery vessel; 5 jade objects; 2 shell beads; 1 turquoise (?) bead; 1 black bead.	
II-11		2 spherical stone objects; 1 bone awl; 1 necklace of canine teeth.	
II-12	In pottery vessel with cover.	Pottery container, shell, and piece of red (hematite) paint.	"Burial" consisted of sawed-off facial portion of skull.
II-13		2 pottery vessels	
II-14	In pottery vessel	Pottery container	Do.
II-15		None	
II-16	In pottery vessel	Pottery container	Do.
II-17	In pottery vessel with cover.	Pottery container	Do.
II-18	Tightly flexed, right side, N. Skull detached, in front of body; mandible also separate. (Decapitated? Secondary burial?).	11 pottery vessels; 56 shell beads; 3 ornamented shells; 5 jade objects; 1 carved turtle shell; 7 shell "rattles"; 1 plain stone yoke; 2 figurines; quantity of red paint.	In center of primary mound. (See Stirling, 1941, pp. 283-286; and pl. 6 of this bulletin.)
II-19	----do----	2 pottery vessels; 2 shell ornaments; clamshells; red paint; 1 bone bead; rodent incisors.	In primary mound.
II-20	Semiextended; skull missing.	1 pottery vessel	In primary mound.

[1] Burials of this series are distinguished by the index numeral II.
[2] The vessels will be described and classified under "Ceramic associations" in table 12, p. 79.

It will be necessary to relate the pottery specimens to the ceramic column from the stratitrenches to resolve this point.

Trench 31 was laid out to cross section a small mound in the large plaza west of the Cerro de las Mesas. It was 15 feet wide and extended clear across the mound in an east-west direction. The completed section of the mound indicated that it, as in the preceding case, consisted of two parts: a small primary mound and a secondary enlargement. No burials were encountered. At the base of the mound, about 72 inches below the crest, and toward the western end of the cut, was a well-preserved stucco floor, a half to three-quarters of an inch thick, 6 feet 3 inches wide by 14 feet 8 inches long (fig. 3; pl. 7, *a*).

The front (west) edge supported three rectangular niches, the rear edge was plain. In the middle of the rear edge was a basin-shaped depression 1 foot in diameter. The floor in front of this pit showed evidence of burning, and the earth underneath was baked to a bright red color. A very similar floor was found in a mound of the Small Mound Locality in the northwest part of the site (trench 14). Beside the basinlike depression stood a flat-bottomed cylindrical pot of ill-fixed coarse paste, which contained a heterogeneous assortment of marine shells, bits of coral, a fragment of fossilized bone, etc., and a jade bead. Stirling remarks that the contents, aside from the bead, looked like the results of a souvenir hunter's half hour on the beach. This was the only complete vessel recovered. Scattered through the mound mass above the floor were numerous sherds of a large apparently zoomorphic pottery figure, and nearer the center of the mound were remnants of another.

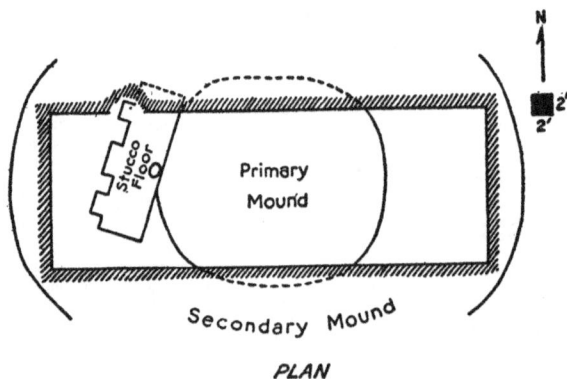

PLAN

FIGURE 3.—Trench 31, plan.

A small cross-trench was put down 72 inches below the floor of the main trench. A few sherds were found throughout the depth of this cut.

Trench 32 was a cross section through another small mound, in the large plaza about 120 feet northwest of trench 31. It was laid out 18 feet wide. This mound, like the preceding, contained but little in the way of structural features. Just east of the center of the mound, the poorly preserved remnants of a floor of clay and stucco (a stucco cap?) were found. The plan of the structure could not be defined.

A large incensario, or the stand of one, was found near the west end of the trench. It had been coated with white stucco, and decorated in red, pink, and black. With it were 6 fire-blackened jade beads and a number of pieces of mica. Two burials were found, the first (II–21) being about 36 inches below the crest of the mound, and the second (II–22) in the east edge about 24 inches deep. II–21 was extended, and accompanied by a small pottery vessel. II–22 was badly disturbed. It had no mortuary offerings.

A cross-trench was sunk below the base of the mound. Sherds from it were segregated from those of the mound mass, and designated by the number of the cut, 32–B.

Trench 33 was a cut 20 feet wide driven into the north end of a large flat-topped mound at the south end of the great plaza of the Central Mound Group (fig. 4). It was not carried through to the heart of the structure, but, in the 30-some feet of its horizontal extent, revealed at least two successive enlargements of the mound. The earlier faces of the structure were equipped with broad stairways (the width of the trench at least), constructed of hard-packed clay (pl. 7, b). The steps are noteworthy for their regularity, varying but slightly from an average rise and tread of 15 inches.

Three burials were uncovered in the course of this excavation. The first two were bundle burials, a type unique at the site. Both were very shallow, and may well have been late intrusions into the

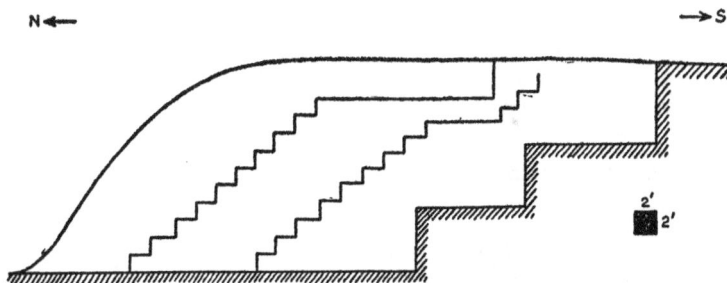

FIGURE 4.—Trench 33, profile, east wall.

mound. II–23 consisted of the incomplete remains of two individuals. With it were two pottery vessels and a small black-painted ball of pottery. II–24 appeared to consist of a single individual, and was accompanied by a small crude pottery vessel. Burial II–25, 44 inches below the front crest of the mound, was also unique, consisting of cremated bones in a small well-baked pit. Above the pit was an ash area 6 feet across. Apparently, after the cremation the pit had been covered and a large bonfire built over it.

Trench 34 was laid out 20 feet wide to give an east-west section of the sizable mound just behind (east of) the monument plaza. When abandoned it had reached a depth of 180 inches below the crest of the mound, with a basal length of 102 feet. This was the trench which produced the tremendously rich jade cache described in detail by Stirling (1941, p. 292 ff.).

The trench, although it did not reach the original ground surface, revealed a section of some complexity. The mound had undergone numerous alterations and enlargements during the period of its use (fig. 5). Three floors of burned earth were uncovered under the middle of the mound, at 30 inches, 38 inches, and 50 inches. Under the third floor were approximately 45 burials in groups of 3 to 8. The skulls were piled together, and the bodies in some instances radiated out from the pile of skulls and in other cases were scattered about promiscuously. The bones were very badly decomposed. Only 2 had any sort of accompanying objects—a large jade bead each. The type of cranial deformation common at the site was noted in all the skulls that were not crushed by the overburden. Some had notched, filed teeth, including one case of a 4-year-old child. Below the level of the burials, a lot of 5 cylindrical flat-bottomed pots of thick poorly fired black paste was found. On the west side of the trench, below the present sloping front of the mound, another series of floors occurred. Beneath a burned earth floor there were 2 floors of stucco, 1 very thin and crumbling, the other thick and well-defined 3 inches deeper. Two

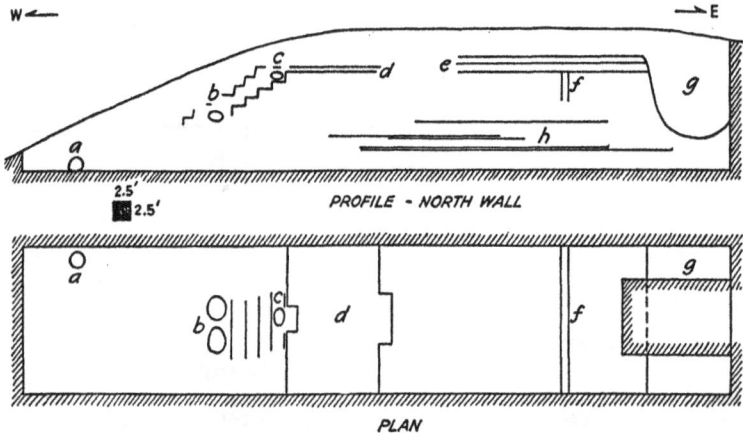

FIGURE 5.—Trench 34: Profile (north wall) and plan. *a*, Jade cache; *b*, Painted stucco fragments; *c*, large idol and pedestal; *d*, stucco floor (and stairway); *e*, burned clay floors; *f*, stucco-faced wall; *g*, pit filled with secondary or disturbed burials; *h*, miscellaneous floors.

bays or niches broke the front and rear edges. In front of the floor a series of stucco-faced steps descended to the west (toward the Monument Plaza) On the steps were several lots of fragments of large figurines, a pile of hollow arms and legs, and below the steps a circle of these objects around a large pot, or, more likely, pedestal of a large idol (pl. 8, *c*, *f*). The pedestal was fitted with a lid with a round hole in the middle, and contained the fragments of a figurine in the form of the body of a flat flabby old male. Below these pieces was the more than life-sized bearded head (pl. 8, *e*).

To the east of the stucco platform occurred a number of flat-based concave-walled tripod vessels, with open bowls as lids. These did not seem to be associated with burials. Each contained several varieties of sea shells, coral, Panama-shell ornaments, sea borer, sand dollar, shark teeth, a fossil, and a large jade bead. One had five jade beads and a Panama shell carved in the form of a face.

East of the stucco floor a stucco-capped wall crossed the trench. Two feet below the top at the east base of this wall was encountered an enormous quantity of coarse White-slipped sherds of more than life-size figures. A group of three child burials was found. One, with filed lower front teeth, had with it a vessel containing a cylindrical stone bead, two Panama-shell ornaments, a sand dollar, and several other marine shells.

The eastern end of the trench cut through a trench or pit which appeared to belong to the same level as the better preserved of the stucco floors. The pit was filled with nondescript mix and great quantities of human bones. It was not possible to determine whether these were secondary burials or whether the dirt collected for filling the pit came from an ancient cemetery.

At a point approximately 96 inches below the crest of the mound and 20 feet down the slope, just under the stairway, occurred several areas of what appeared to be layers of paint. The largest was roughly rectangular, 1 foot 8 inches wide by 2 feet 7 inches long. We at first considered the material to be remnants of codices, but later revised our opinion, in view of the complete absence of any traces of backing. In all probability, the find represents a painted structural feature, perhaps a wall or the front of a collapsed clay altar.[3] The dozen or so layers of paint were directly one on top of the other. The weight of the overburden had not only completely crushed and cracked the delicate substance, but had driven clods and pebbles completely through it, making it impossible to recover anything but small fragments. The paints appeared to be of the same origin as the "stucco" paints applied to some of the vessels from the grave lots in trench 30. Bright red, green, and white served as base or background colors (each in a different layer), and as well for what appeared to be small-element designs painted on them. Black was frequently used to outline the design elements. A few traces of a dark purplish-blue paint were noted. Beneath the paint areas were masses of human bone, apparently secondary burials, portions of which extended into and through the paint.

In removing the north wheelbarrow ramp in the northwest corner of the trench some heavy incensario fragments were encountered. Under these and a heavy, rough slab of cement was a cache of about 800 objects of jade,[4] including many large circular earplugs, figurines, gorgets, tubes, beads, etc. These exhibited a wide variety of style

---

[3] Compare the fresco decoration of Cempoala, in Seler, 1915, pp. 145 ff.
[4] This find has been described in detail by Stirling (1941, pp. 292 ff.).

and material: "Olmec" faces, danzantes, axes, canoes, "Oaxaca circles," and similar objects in almost infinite variety. The only objects in the lot not of jade were a stone monkey figure painted red, 16 inches high and 7 inches wide; a small standing human figure of black stone; and a stone turtle painted red. A celt and a sphere were made of translucent green alabaster.

The bottom of the cache was 6 feet below the surface and no indication of an intrusive pit was visible (pl. 8, *c*, *e*, *f*).

Trenches 2, 4, 10, 11, 13, 17, 18, 20, 21, 22, 23, 24, 25, and 26 compose a system of excavations designed to test thoroughly the sherd-bearing zone in the level open plain to the north of the Central Mound Group. The first four (2, 4, 10, and 11) were laid out at random; 2, 4, and 10 were test pits 5 by 15 feet in horizontal dimension; 11 was started as a stratitest, 10 by 40 feet, but abandoned at the conclusion of the 24- to 36-inch level. Trench 13 was laid out 10 feet north-south by 40 feet east-west, adjacent to trench 10, and was dug as a stratitest, in 12-inch levels. The remaining trenches of the system were tests laid out at 100-foot intervals on the north–south and east-west axes of a datum set up at the southwest corner of trench 13. These last were all 6 feet wide by 10 feet long. The sketch map (fig. 1) shows the relationships of the units of this system.

The results of these cuts (excepting, for the moment, the stratitest) have been summarized in the comparison of former and present landscapes in the discussion of the deposits. A more detailed account will be given here coupled with a series of diagrams. The most noteworthy fact is that the sherd-bearing horizon varied considerably, and irregularly, in depth at the points tested. The preoccupational landscape differed from that of the present day as the result of continued soil deposition. The level plain of today, whose monotony is interrupted only by man-made earth-mounds, is superimposed on an ancient rolling landscape. The following tabulation of trench depths will make this point clear (the sequence of trenches is from north-south, and east–west, along the axes laid out from the datum at the southwest corner of trench 13):

Trench No.	Maximum depth of sherd-bearing soil (inches)	Trench No.	Maximum depth of sherd-bearing soil (inches)
N 22	71–92	E 25	[1]100–116
↑ 21	48–53	↑ 24	[2] 99–128
20	27–32	23	47–48
13	40–122	13	40–122
10	135–145+	↓ 17	50–56
↓ 26	54–68	W 18	30
S 2	60–61		

[1] 0–42 inches sterile.
[2] 0–36 to 40 inches sterile.

It is noteworthy that even within the few feet of horizontal area of the individual trenches the depth of the subsoil varies. Very likely the ancient surface was even more irregular and rolling than the schematic section (fig. 6) indicates.

This change in physiography from past to present is significant on varied counts. For our present purposes, it means that stratigraphic results from the locality must be used with caution. A filled-in hollow in a hilly terrain is not the same thing as a gradually, and more or less uniformly built-up occupational deposit or midden. This is especially true where the precise areal extent of the "hollow" is not known. The structure of the subsoil as well as that of the deposit must be known to permit analysis of the results. The deepest soil structure encountered (trenches 2, 10, 13, 17, 18, 24) was a heavy clayey dark purplish-brown material, completely sterile of cultural debris. Although levels were not run with instrument, the upper surface of this soil in the several cuts appeared to follow a very

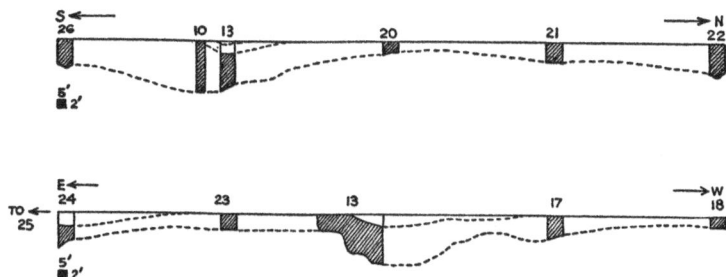

FIGURE 6.—Sections through area of sherd deposits.

nearly horizontal plane; similarly, in the largest section uncovered (trench 13), there was no perceptible dip. In all probability, this formation is an ancient swamp muck. Superimposed on it are various light soils, composed mainly of fine sands. The predominant colors are yellow to yellowish brown, but lenses of clean gray sand occur. These are the formations or irregular surface. The sections as revealed in the trenches give the impression of dunelike structures. It is worthy of mention that Stirling (1943, p. 31) noted active sand dunes in the low swampy "El Coyol" region 15 or 20 miles eastward, toward the Bay of Alvarado. Apparently, the land along the west shore has been encroaching gradually on the bay, first by sedimentation and formation of swamp, and then by wind-borne sand. The occupancy of Cerro de las Mesas evidently began after the locality had begun to assume its islandlike character owing to deposition of sand. The problem of water supply, in the early periods at least, was not a pressing one, for in places culture-bearing soils lie directly on the ancient swamp muck (trenches 10, 13). In the gullies between the dunes there must have been innumerable streamlets.

Aggradation did not cease with the beginning of human occupancy. The "deposits" differ from the dune soils only in their addition of cultural debris—sherds, charcoal and ash, animal bone, and the like. Of course, the concentration of cultural material varies; there are lenses and pockets of nearly pure debris and but little sand. For the most part, however, the proportion of soil is much greater than that of the sherds etc. The chief difference to be noted is in the type of deposition. Instead of forming irregular, and presumably traveling dunes, there was a tendency to fill depressions and in general level off the land surface. One can only guess to what extent human agencies were responsible for this change. It is not unlikely that the houses and perhaps milpas, and the dumping of animal refuse (which would stimulate plant growth) were potent factors in "anchoring" the dunes and leveling off the plain. This leveling process has continued to the present, as the sterile caps overlying the deposit in some places (trenches 24 and 25) demonstrate.

The uppermost soil division of the present series has little if any archeological significance. It is basically the same as the soils which it overlies: light, sandy, in most places in the sherd locality culture-bearing, but distinguished by its darker grayish color. This color difference is owing to the presence of humic materials, presumably accumulated since cessation of the aboriginal occupation. In view of the prevailing light soil type of the region, the depth to which these materials have been washed down (11 to 18 inches) cannot be taken as indicative of a long period of abandonment; much less so when the modern type of cultivation—plowing—is brought into consideration.

To summarize, occupation of the locality began at a time when the site was covered by rolling dunes. In the formation of the deposits a natural process of aggradation was involved, in addition to the accumulation of cultural refuse. Consequently, isolated examples of thick deposits cannot be construed as indicative of great age, for deposition of this sort is probably relatively rapid, at least as compared with processes of soil formation such as were observed in the deposits at Tres Zapotes.

Trench 13, 40 feet east-west by 10 north-south, was dug as a strati-trench, that is to say, in foot-levels to a depth of 144 inches. The completed section revealed a profile consisting of several culture-bearing strata with a uniform westward dip, owing chiefly to the marked dip of sterile layers on which they rested, despite the fact that the present ground surface runs nearly level (fig. 7). The culture-bearing levels consisted of light sandy buff to grayish-brown soils containing sherds and miscellaneous refuse. They differed among themselves chiefly in their content of charcoal, ash, and similar substances, which caused the color differentiation. The principal exception was a thick layer of rich greasy-looking dark-brown mix extending downward from 45 inches. This zone averaged 30 to 36 inches in thickness. It contained, in addition to quantities of sherds, 17 large vessels, complete or nearly so, most of them being Plain ware ollas.

The profile is at first glance complicated by several intrusive pits which extended downward from the black level and the member below it into the basic soil zone. The purpose of these pits was not apparent; they contained nothing but mix in the portions investigated. In addition to a few stray human bones, four burials were found in the trench, I-2, I-3, I-4, and I-5, and one, I-6, in a shoveling platform at the east end of the cut.

The trench 13 section clearly represents a dump of refuse in a sizable hollow on a gully in the original terrain. Despite the con-

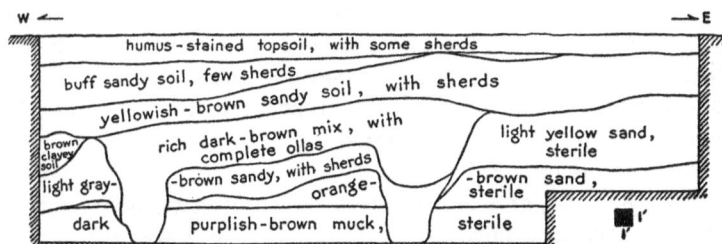

FIGURE 7.—Trench 13, profile, north wall.

siderable depth of the major part of this deposit, there is no real evidence that a very long time interval was involved in this filling-in process. Furthermore, in view of the fact that the horizontal stratigraphic levels dug do not conform to the natural planes of the deposit, the sherd counts from the trench cannot be expected to be as sensitive to ceramic change as might be desired. However, they do show certain gross trends which corroborate results from other investigations at the site.

Ten burials (if we include two secondary or badly disturbed ones) were encountered in this series of excavations. The data recorded are summarized in table 3.

This small sampling of burials presents several points of interest, especially in view of the fact that evidence from the stratigraphic levels can be adduced to show that all belong to the same general period. First and most striking is the complete absence of any pattern of burial position or orientation. Second, we may note the paucity of grave offerings—this is the more striking when contrasted

TABLE 3.—*Summary of data on 10 burials found in trenches 4, 13, 22, 23, and 25*

Burial No.[1]	Trench No.	Depth [2] (inches)	Position and orientation	Associations	Remarks
I-1	4	60	Semiflexed, dorsal, knees originally raised. WNW.	River clamshell over mouth.	Plate 13, *a.*
I-2	13	39	(Secondary or disturbed)__	None_____	Incomplete (plate 13, *b*).
I-3	13	48	Semiflexed, left side. E.	River clamshell in mouth; 4 small pottery vessels.	Plate 13, *c.*
I-4	13	56	Extended, ventral. W.	River clamshell over mouth.	Plate 13, *d.*
I-5	13	60	Tight-flexed, ventral. N.	River clamshell near mouth.	Plate 13, *e.*
I-6	[3] 13	27	Tight (?) flexed, dorsal. W.	____do_____	Legs missing (feet in place close to pelvis). Plate 13, *f.*
I-7	23	40	Tight-flexed, ventral. SSW.	2 white stone beads at cervical region.	Plate 14, *a.*
I-8	22	75	Extended, ventral. S.	None_____	Plate 14, *b.*
I-9	22	62	Tight-flexed, dorsal. E.	____do_____	Plate 14, *c.*
I-15	25	110–116	(Secondary or disturbed).	____do_____	In sandy subsoil at base of deposit.

[1] Burials found in the test and stratigraphic trenches are indicated within index No. I.
[2] Depth measurements to skull.
[3] Encountered in shoveling platform at east end of trench, not in trench proper.

with the burials from the mounds. However, there is one important detail which serves to connect these burials with those of the mounds: the custom of placing a shell near or over the mouth. As has been mentioned, this trait was noted in several instances in the mound burials (trench 30), and doubtless represents a variation of the ceremonial use of shells, represented by the offerings of shells previously described (pp. 8, 9).

Trenches 3, 5, 27, and 28 were tests laid out some 500 yards west of trench 2, etc., in a north-south line. Trench 3 was the southernmost; trench 5 was laid out 250 yards to the north. Trenches 27 and 28 were laid out at 100-foot intervals south of the southwest corner of trench 5 to check the nature of the deposit.

This series of trenches revealed a deposit of the same type as that found in the previously described system, in fact, probably a continuation of the same structure. Cultural material occurred in soil of the same type, and beneath the sherd layers were encountered sterile formations apparently identical to those underlying the deposits already described. The same sort of irregular preoccupational surface appeared, as the following tabulation of depth of deposit shows:

	Trench No.	Maximum depth of sherd-bearing soil (inches)
N	5_____	[1] 76–81
↑	27_____	[2] 80–86
	28_____	88–92
	3_____	60–63

[1] 0–38 inches sterile.
[2] 0–43 inches sterile.

It should be added that the sherd horizon of trench 5 appeared to be a unit structure of a uniform dark-brown color, middenlike in appearance. In trench 27 this horizon was but 10 to 16 inches thick (38 to 48 (north end), 54 (south end)); in trench 28, 14 inches (43 to 57). Below were layers with only a few sherds. In trench 3 sherds were scarce below 48 inches.

A third group of trenches was dug in the Small Mound Locality to the northwest of the last series of trenches described. The locality was selected after a field appraisal of the ceramics recovered particularly from the stratitrench 13. It was noted that wares of the Polychrome group, known from surface collections from the site, were rare in the materials excavated in the stratitest and the adjacent test pits. Since Polychrome sherds were found to occur in abundance on the (plowed) surface of the Small Mound Locality at the northwest end of the site, several trenches were laid out: 14 (and 14–A), 19, 40, 41, and 42. All but the last were mound cuts. The most important point to be noted is that two of the cuts, 19 and 41, showed that the mounds overlay refuse deposits of some thickness. The terrain in this locality is quite irregular, what with the hodgepodge of small mounds, borrow-pits, and gullies. Just to the north the present land surface dips toward the low-lying "potreros" that surround the site. All in all, the locality is by no means prepossessing. However, it was just here that the thickest and most important depositional horizon was found. Trench 42, dug as a stratitest to section the submound layers revealed by trenches 19 and 41, disclosed 15 feet of nearly horizontally laid refuse layers, or over 17 feet (209 inches) if subsoil irregularities are taken into account (pl. 12). This section is by far the most important of the Cerro de las Mesas excavations, for it proved to contain the most nearly complete series of sherds, a series which appears to cover the entire period of occupation of the site.

Trenches 14 and 14–A were dug on a small irregularly shaped mound, or more likely a composite mound (fig. 8). Trench 14 uncovered a stucco floor, presumably of a ceremonial structure. The floor originally extended across the southeastern crown of the mound, but its southern end could not be followed, owing to the destructive effects of the roots of a large tree. At its center, the floor was covered by 14 or 15 inches of dirt; its northern edge and part of the eastern one were plowed out, being less deeply covered owing to the dip of the mound. Where better protected, the floor turned up 5 or 6 inches at the edges, forming in that fashion the base of the walls. The floor itself consisted of a number of layers of stucco of sand and slaked shells. Some of the layers showed traces of red paint. In form long and narrow, the floor had two bays or enclosed rectangles on its west side reminiscent of those of the stucco floor found in trench 31 (fig. 3). On the east side directly between the two was a smaller rectangle with rounded corners, faced and floored on the inside, 9 inches below the level of the floor. It was filled with ash. On each side were circular pits, likewise stuccoed on the interior, one 41 and the other 42 inches deep. They contained nothing but dirt.

On the west side of the mound, descending from a low crown, was a row of pipe made of coarse unslipped ware (pl. 10, c). The joints were 1 foot 8 inches to 2 feet long, 7 to 9 inches in diameter, with one belled and one plain end so that they telescoped neatly. Unfortunately, the line of pipe had been badly broken up in plowing the mound, but enough remained to show an original length of about

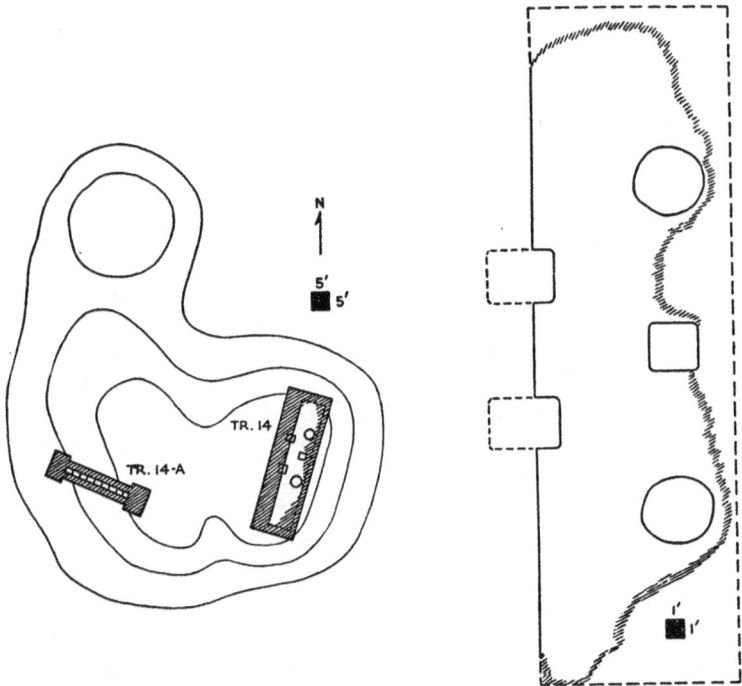

FIGURE 8.—Trenches 14 and 14–A, and detail of floor, trench 14.

18 feet, with a dip of about 3 feet in this distance. There was no evidence of a structure at either end.

Trench 41 was dug in a small mound about 100 feet due south of trench 40. The cut was 10 feet wide by 25 feet north-south. It was carried to a maximum of 208 inches below the peak of the mound, except for a small block left in the north end to support remnants of structures.

Despite its small size, the mound had been rebuilt several times. Four well-defined floors, three of them of stucco, in the uppermost 38 inches of the mound, and three superimposed stucco facings at the north end demonstrate this point (fig. 9). 105 inches below the crest was an inch-thick floor of stucco, painted bright red, and lying on a prepared base of gray sand. The north end of this feature tailed off into rubble of stucco and large incensario sherds. This point seems to represent the original base of the mound. Below was a culture-bearing deposit seemingly of primary type, which was more thoroughly investigated by a stratitrench (trench 42), and, therefore, need not be described in detail here.

In addition to stray fragments of human bone found at various points in the mound mass and the inferior layers as well, two burials were uncovered, I–12 and I–13. Both seemed to belong to the earlier (though not earliest) phases of the mound's construction. Both were remains of children, and in a lamentable state of preservation. The most important feature is the association of a small quantity of copper

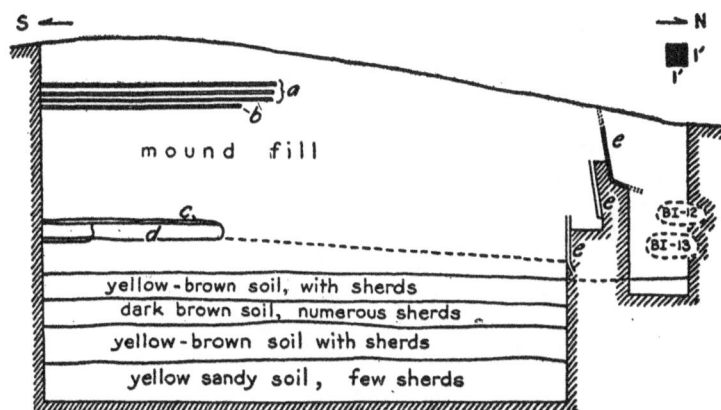

FIGURE 9.—Trench 41: Profile (west wall). *a*, Stucco floors; *b*, sand and clay floor; *c*, red-painted stucco floor; *d*, rubble of stucco and sherds; *e*, stucco wall-facings; BI-12, burial I-12; BI-13, burial I-13.

ornaments with I–13—the only pre-Hispanic metal found on the site.

Trench 19 was dug 30 feet east-west by 15 feet north-south, in the west end of a double mound of the Small Mound Group. The excavation was put down to 110 inches, with a reduced cut 4 feet wide dug 36 inches more along the south wall of the trench. Remnants of a number of structures, representing different periods of construction, were encountered, though it must be owned that the original plans could not be worked out within the confines of the trench. Disintegrated stucco floors appeared at 11 and at 30 inches. At 18 inches appeared a stucco layer 11 feet east-west, descending in two steps to the west, and rising at its eastern end. At 60 to 73 inches were stucco-faced walls and piers of at least three structures. (See fig. 10.) Most curious was the clay-lined pit 3 feet wide by 7 long and 15 inches deep, filled with clean gray sand. This feature seemed to belong to one of the structures. Layers of similar sand 2 to 3 inches thick were noted in the south side of the trench at 48, and at 79 inches. The mound at a depth of from 70 to 84 inches consisted of irregular and interrupted areas of burned earth, etc. Presumably these were the

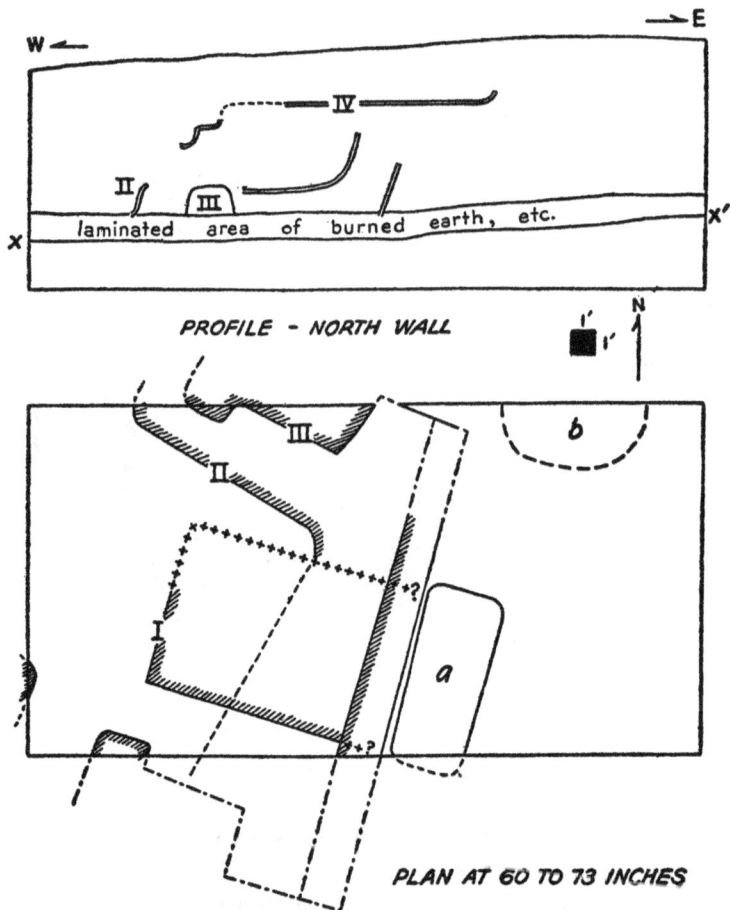

FIGURE 10.—Trench 19: Profile (north wall) and plan at 60 to 73 inches. *a*, Clay-lined pit filled with gray sand; *b*, pit filled with fragments of Monumental ware. I–IV, Structures with stucco-faced walls. Numerical order corresponds to order of construction. Shading indicates inner side of stuccoed walls. x–x' (in profile), probable base of mound.

floor associated with one and another of the structures, and represent the top of the original low platform. The base of this structure was not certainly defined, but appeared to lie at a level 85 to 89 inches deep. Below this point sherds were markedly less numerous than in the mound mass, and the level corresponds pretty well to the overall height of the mound above the present ground surface.

In the course of the excavation, two lots of fragments of large incensarios, etc., were found, one near the northeast corner of the trench at 64 inches, the other in the west end, in an intrusive pit 2½ feet across, whose point of origin lay between 80 and 84 inches and extended to a depth of 108 inches. The pit contained quantities of charcoal and ash, and the sherds themselves showed evidence of having been burned. Five burials were recovered from the cut as well, I–10, I–11, I–17, I–18, and I–19. The three latter were all infant burials, interred in sizable ollas covered with bowls. Burial I–11 is of most interest because it lay in a concave round object (a wooden or gourd bowl?) painted with the same bright "stucco" paint as was found in trench 34. The burial lay below the mound mass proper, with no clear evidence of intrusion from above. At the depth of 100 inches was an irregular layer of paint, too fragmentary to be saved. Directly below lay the skull and ribs of the (secondary) burial, on top of a pile of long bones. Beneath, serving as a container apparently, was the object previously mentioned, with a central design in white, green, and black on a bright red background. A painting of the design is reproduced in figure 209.

Trench 40 was staked out as a small mound, just to the west of trench 19, in an extension of the same mound. The cut was enlarged to remove the chief find, a cache of covered pots containing skulls. This peculiar deposit has been described by Stirling (1941, pp. 289–290) ; all that need be done here is to summarize the main facts. A few inches below the surface, so shallow, in fact, that the upper portions had been badly shattered by plowing, were 6 pots containing bone fragments, apparently of skulls.[5] Below, at a depth of 16 inches, was a layer of stucco, 61 feet long north-south by 14 feet 8 inches wide. At the northeast corner was a rectangular extension 7 feet 3 inches long by 6 feet 6 inches across. The floor dipped about a foot from the middle toward either end. At the middle of the western edge of the floor was a double row of pots covered with bowls, each containing a skull and three or four cervical vertebrae. The double row contained 24 vessels, with two more just to the east at the south end (pl. 11). A good number of the skulls were of subadults and children. At 26 inches was another stucco floor, 14 feet 11 inches wide, its east and west edges corresponding pretty closely with those of the upper one. Its north-south extent was not determined. At a point almost directly below the first double row of pots, below the second floor, was another double row of covered vessels of the same size and type, likewise containing skulls and cervical vertebrae. There were 22 pots in this lot. Beneath,

---

[5] There may have been more of these vessels originally. Local people informed me that a number of years ago, a house stood on the mound, and that the owner, in setting the posts, etc., had found several "pots with bones." Since some time had elapsed since the house had gone to ruin and the trees had been cleared from the mound, no one was quite sure whether the house stood in the vicinity of trench 40 or nearer trench 19, to the east.

at 56 inches, was a third stucco floor, 15 feet 9 inches across. Its east and west edges extended a few inches beyond those of the superior floors. Near the middle of this floor, opposite the area of the pots, was a circular hole 3 feet 5 inches in diameter, which contained nothing suggesting its purpose. Below, no other structures were found to a depth of 80 inches, at which point the cut was abandoned. When concluded, the trench had a horizontal area of 20 by 20 feet, with the addition of the cleared uppermost floor. It should be noted that aside from the floors and the skull pots, the mound was very nearly sterile, there being scarcely any sherds in the mound mass.

Several facts combine to indicate that the trench 40 find represents a unit deposit, that is to say, that the three floors were laid, and the pots with their grisly contents were deposited all in one operation. Most convincing is the close correspondence of location of floors and rows of pots. The marked similarity in size and form of the vessels of the three levels points to the same conclusion, as does the nearly uniform state of preservation of the skulls of the two lower levels (the plow-shattered fragments of the uppermost lot cannot in fairness be compared with the rest).

Trench 42 was staked out 30 feet north-south by 10 feet east-west, in the open flat adjacent to the mounds in which the other cuts of this series were put. An arbitrary datum (0–0') was established across the irregular (plowed) surface, to facilitate measurement. The uppermost 48 inches consisted of a finely divided yellowish-brown sandy soil, with sherds and miscellaneous refuse. This horizon had a humus-stained topsoil, likewise sherd-bearing, 16 to 20 inches thick. Within the horizon were two floors of packed sand, an inch to an inch and a half in thickness. That these were prepared floors, probably of dwellings, was demonstrated by the fact that one was definitely associated with a clearly marked firepit, a portion of which remained in the west wall of the trench. (See profile, fig. 11.) This floor, the upper of the two, occurred at 33 to 34 inches; the lower at 46 to 47.

Beneath this zone lay one nearly identical in color and texture, distinguished chiefly by its very low sherd content. It extended to a depth of 94 to 114 inches, at which point it overlay another horizon lighter in color but likewise poor in cultural material. This layer extended to 134 to 139 inches. Under this latter occurred a layer of dark-brown soil, rich and "greasy" in appearance, with a very high sherd yield. Charcoal, ash, animal bone, etc., likewise had a high frequency. This horizon lay directly on the sterile subsoil, a yellow clayey formation with pockets and lenses of gray sand, at a depth ranging from 178 to 188 inches.

Evidences of disturbance were few. All of those noted occurred in the lowest depositional horizon—the dark-brown middenlike mix. At

157 inches, in the southwest corner of the trench, a circular firepit, roughly 3 feet in diameter and 8 to 10 inches in depth, filled with small water-worn stones 1½ to 4 inches in diameter, charcoal, ash, etc., was found. At 180 inches, in midtrench, appeared another hearth. This one was rectangular with rounded corners, 3 feet 5 inches long by 1 foot 10 inches wide, and 5 to 6 inches deep. In the northwest corner of the trench, in fact, running under the north wall, was a burial, I–16 (pl. 14, f). The uppermost point of the skull was at 184½ inches, the pelvis at 187. This burial belongs to the very earliest occupation of this locality, for it lay in the sterile clayey subsoil.

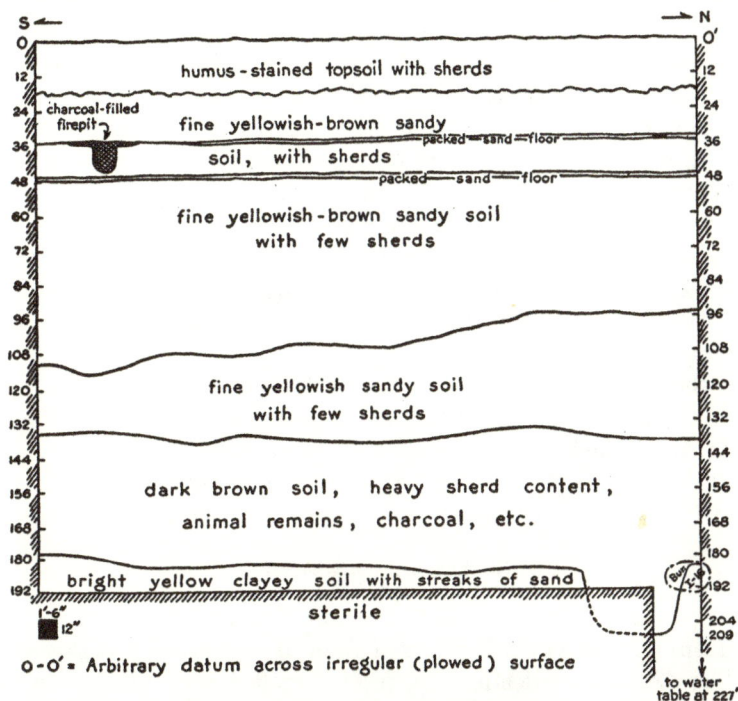

FIGURE 11.—Trench 42, profile, west wall.

A later intrusive pit from the dark-brown horizon cut off the lower legs of the skeleton. This pit, whose point of origin could not be defined with precision, save that it lay within the lowermost soil zone, extended to a depth of 209 inches.

To summarize, the section disclosed in trench 42 was of a deep deposit, with but few and localized disturbances, whose lower and upper layers indicate fairly intensive human occupation. The phases represented by the middle layers suggest less intensive occupation of the locality (i e., as though the center of habitation had shifted slightly) or a period of more rapid aggradation. There is, however, no indication of a clean break, or an unconformity in the horizons, a fact corroborated by the ceramic evidence.

Trench 43 was not, properly speaking, a trench. It consisted of a discovery pit made by some local people in the process of digging gophers, of a "pipe-line" similar to that of trench 14–A, and a quantity of figurines. The find occurred in a small mound about a quarter of a mile south-southwest of the trench series, 19, 40, 41, and 42, belonging to the same Small Mound Locality. The sections of pipe, similar to those of trench 14–A, angled down the northeast side of the mound. The uppermost joint was modeled to represent a female human torso. The head is missing. Over the end of this was set another incomplete figure, apparently part of an elaborate incensario. Quantities of Polychrome sherds and other figurines occurred along with this lot of material.

Trench 6 was dug 15 feet north-south by 6 feet east-west in a small mound about 8 feet high on top of a large platform mound of the Western Group. The locality was suggested by the reported finding of a small stone yoke in the small mound just previous to the arrival of the expedition. However, the attempt proved fruitless. A scant handful of sherds were found, and no other material at all from the cut, which extended to a maximum depth (from the peak of the mound) of 94 inches.

Of the remaining test cuts, 1, 8, and 9, there is little to be said, for none tapped refuse deposits of any consequence. All were dug in localities in which sherds appeared on the surface, but in no case did cultural remains extend more than a few inches down into the humus-stained topsoil. Beneath lay undisturbed and sterile soil zones.

CERRO DE LAS MESAS WARES

The pottery of Cerro de las Mesas classifies out in a somewhat peculiar fashion. Strict application of the ware criterion that served for the Tres Zapotes collections (a high correlation of paste, slip, and vessel shapes) gives us but two ceramic groups: one a numerically small but quite distinct body of material, and the other including all the rest of the local pottery. This latter must be broken down according to variations of slipping, painting, and the like, to give serviceable units for comparative and stratigraphic analyses. The point is that the major portion of the local ceramics conforms to a single pattern of paste type, vessel shapes, and, to a considerable extent, slip. This focal type is that of Brown ware, i. e., of coarse, sand-tempered paste, with a tendency to thick walls, and slipped with a pigment apparently made of the same clay as the paste. Red ware is essentially the same ware with an all-over coat of red paint (overlying a brown wash or slip). Another variant, Red-on-Brown, has the red pigment distributed in patterns instead of all over. The various Black wares, Black, and Black-and-White, are like Brown in paste and vessel shapes, and in use of a slip of the same clay as that of the paste. The same incised designs occur on Black and on Brown vessels. The difference appears to be solely one of firing technique, by means of which paste and slip attain a black instead of a brown color. Several varieties of Polychrome as well are essentially Brown ware with multicolor painted decoration.

It is consequently necessary to abandon the ideologically more consistent system of classification for one more applicable to the material at hand. As may be gathered from the preceding paragraph, the main criterion of classification is slip and/or paint. The ceramic groups thus segregated have been designated for convenience "wares," and will be described under separate heads in the following section.

The recurrence in most of these ceramic units of the same vessel shapes makes possible a few generalizations with respect to the dominant form patterns. There is a wide range of elaborate shapes, but numerically these comprise only a small proportion of the determinable types. Simple silhouette vessels tending toward broad, rather squat, proportions are most common. The chief type of rim is the simple direct one. Scale drawings of vessel types and rims accompany the section in which the shapes are described. It should be noted, however, that certain of the more elaborate forms are based on one or two complete specimens only, preserved, for example, in grave offerings, and should be considered neither common nor typical of local ceramics. The prevailing pattern is one of simple shapes.

While the small size of the majority of sherds from the stratigraphic sections renders unsatisfactory attempts at distributions of shape types, there are certain elements of form which are temporarily significant. These will be discussed in connection with the stratigraphic analyses.

UNTEMPERED WARE

Throughout a considerable part of the ceramic history of the site there occurs a ware which is distinct from other local wares in nearly every respect. It is composed of a very finely divided paste, quite hard, with little or no visible temper. Paste colors range from buff to light orange, with a small proportion of sherds with a steel-gray core, and fewer, steel-gray through and through. Vessel walls tend to be thin. The most common slip is one of the same clay as the paste, fired to the same shade as to outer portions of the walls. There is also a slip of different origin, which fires from a white to cream color, and is applied in a thick coat which gives a lacquerlike appearance. In many instances vestiges of painted designs remain. For this reason the ware is considered as one type of Polychrome.

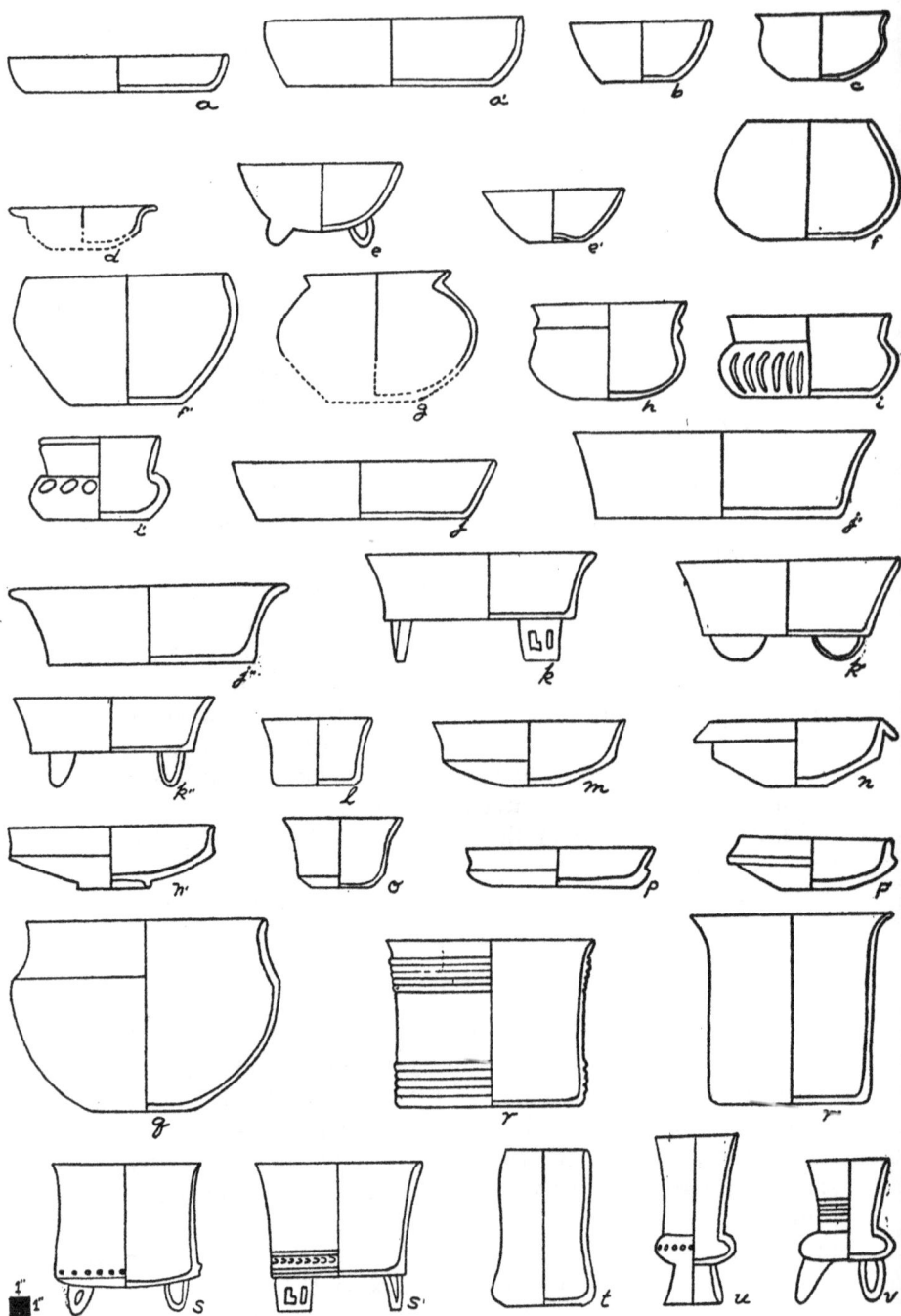

FIGURE 12.—Form types of Cerro de las Mesas wares.
(For description of vessel shapes, see pp. 60–61.)

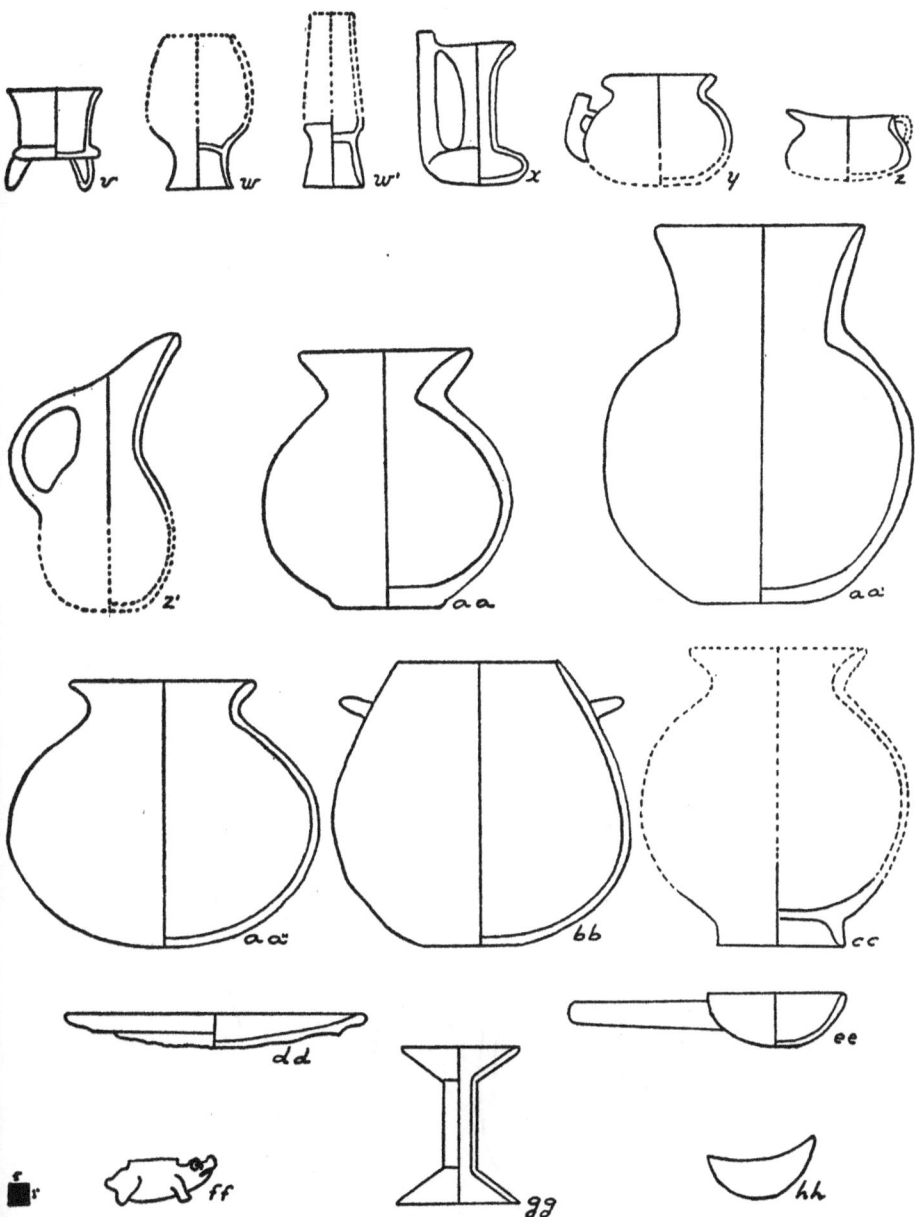

FIGURE 12.—Continued.

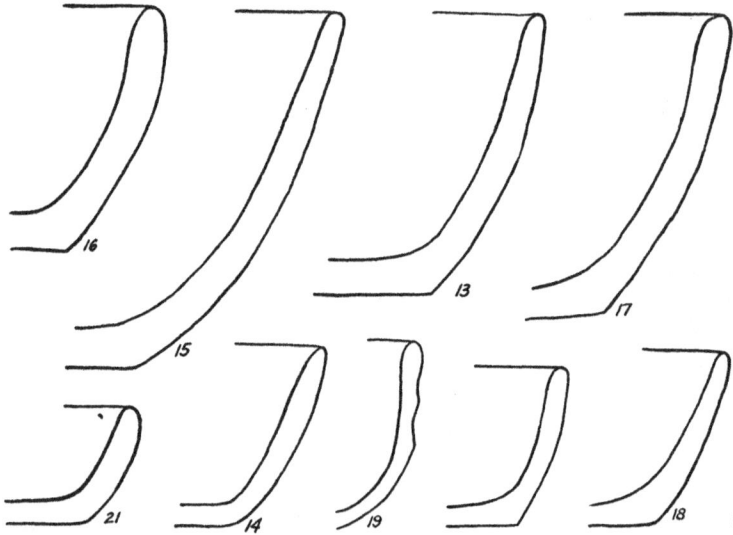

FIGURES 13–21.—Rims of vessel form-types *a*, *a'*, *b*, *e*, and *e'* (shown in figure 12).

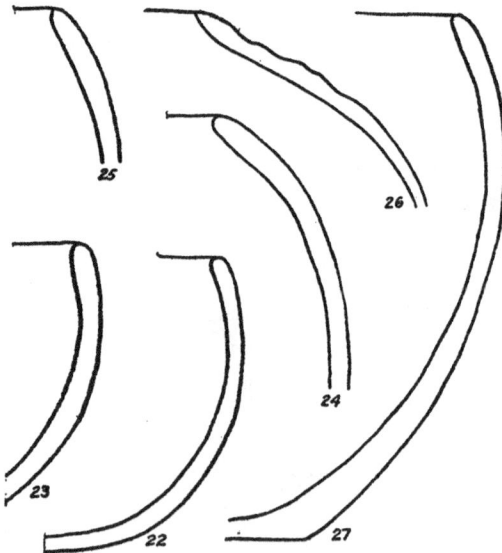

FIGURES 22–27.—Rims of vessel form-types *f*, *f'* (shown in figure 12).

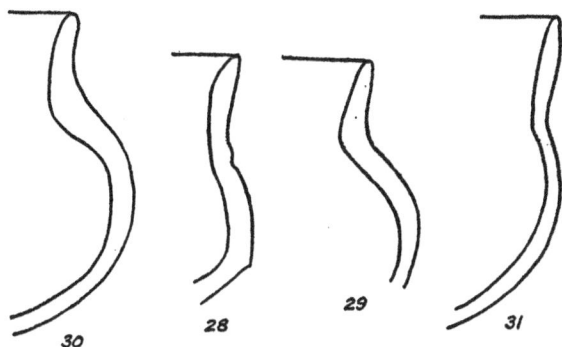

FIGURES 28–31.—Rims of vessel form-types *h* and *i* (shown in figure 12).

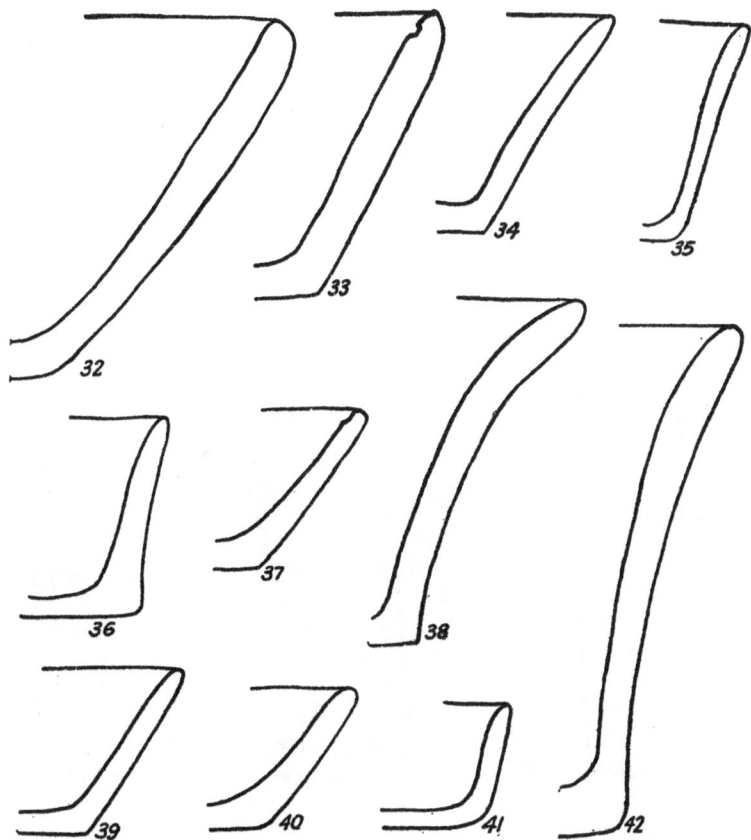

FIGURES 32–42.—Rims of vessel form-types *j* to *l* (shown in figure 12).

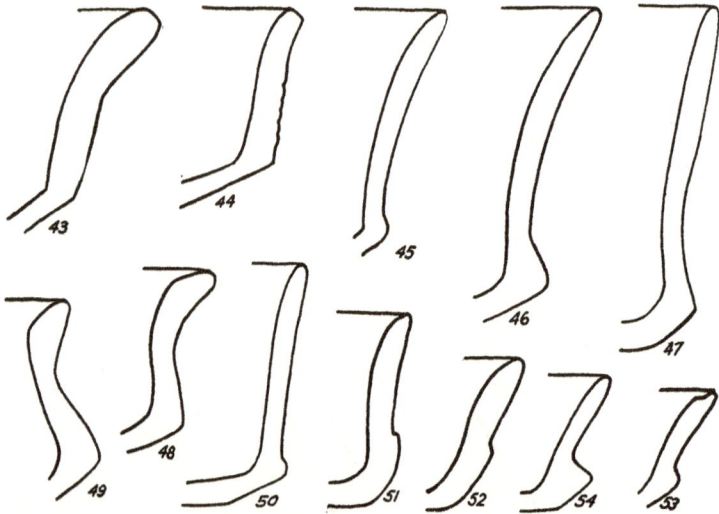

FIGURES 43–54.—Rims of vessel form-types *m* to *p'* (shown in figure 12).

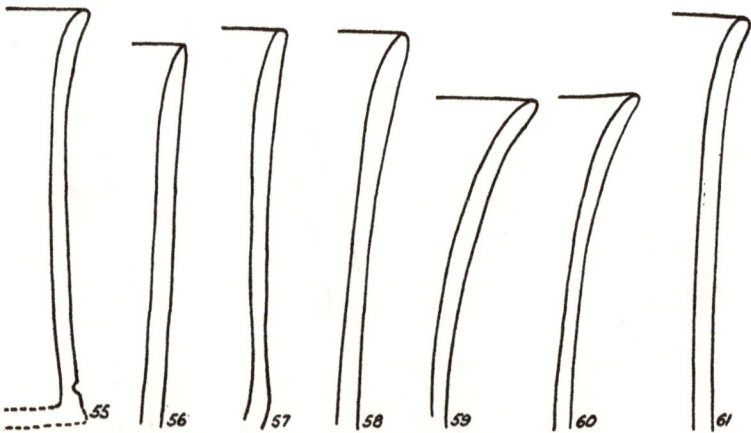

FIGURES 55–61.—Rims of vessel form-types *r* to *v'* (shown in figure 12).

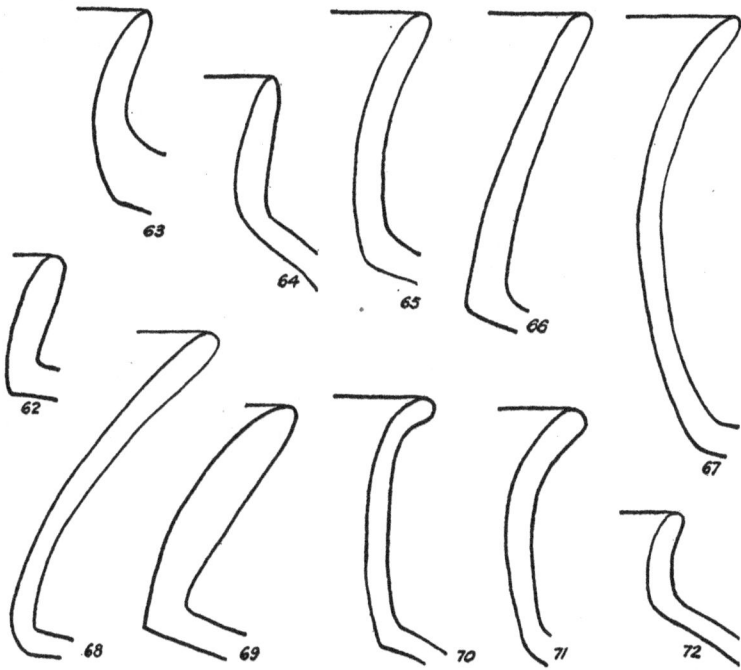

FIGURES 62–72.—Rims of vessel form-types *aa* to *aa''* (shown in figure 12).

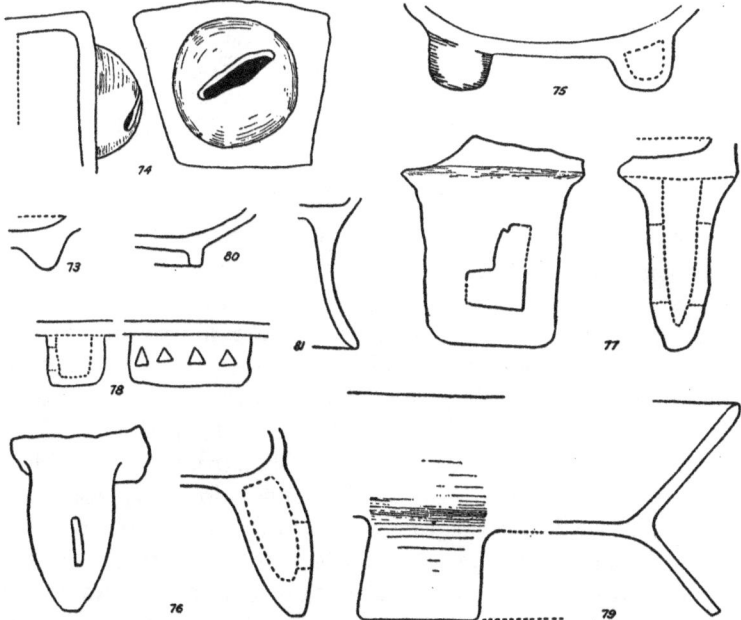

FIGURES 73–81.—Types of vessel supports: Figure 73, solid knob feet; 74, broad hemispherical hollow feet; 75, small hollow feet; 76, elongate cylindrical to flattened hollow legs; 77, hollow slab legs; 78, modified hollow slab legs (properly, feet); 79, thin solid slab legs; 80, low annular base; 81, tall annular base.

The writer believes this ware to be a manifestation of a ceramic type widely distributed both in time and space in the Veracruz area. On the one hand, it is represented by the Tres Zapotes Polychromes, and on the other, by a number of late Veracruz types, such as the wares designated Cerro Montoso, or "Totonac." It even seems likely that the well-known Fine Orange belongs to this same class. Not only is there correspondence in the type of paste (which indicates a technology distinct from that of other wares of the region), but, as well, certain shapes suggestive of that of classic Fine Orange occur in the Untempered ware, and the combination of incising and painting for decorative effect also occurs.

Because of the relatively small quantity of this ware at Cerro de las Mesas, but few vessel forms are definable. It may be noted that despite unquestionable identities in paste and slip, typical Tres Zapotes Polychrome shapes do not occur, although there are some resemblances.

Little can be said as to decorative motifs of this ware, owing to the combined circumstances of the perishable nature of the paints and the small size of the sherds in the collections. Various combinations of red, orange, and black were painted on, but the paints either were of a perishable sort, or could not penetrate the hard glossy surfaces of the vessels. Little more than smudges remain. In addition, both prefiring and post-firing incising was often applied, apparently to supplement or accent painted patterns. Herein lies one of the major differences between this ware and Tres Zapotes Polychrome (where incised decoration is quite rare), and a similarity to Fine Orange, even though the boldly carved panels sometimes seen in the latter seem to be lacking.

BROWN WARE

Cerro de las Mesas Brown ware is distinguished by its slip color, which ranges from a bright orange brown to dark brick red to a dark chocolate. Occasional sherds lack the reddish tones and tend to olive browns. As a rule Brown ware vessels are not evenly fired, but tend to be mottled with firing clouds, or darker on one side than on the other. Ordinarily, the surfaces of vessels of this ware are fairly well polished, except in the case of the unslipped bases of bowls.

The characteristic paste is only moderately hard, with a considerable quantity of sand temper. It has the same color range as the slip. Frequently there is a black core, presumably from imperfect firing. It should be noted that vessel walls tend to be relatively thick.

Now and again one finds a sherd with a mixture of sand and shell temper instead of sand alone. Such pieces seem to occur at all periods. It is not possible to determine if they represent deliberate attempts at use of another tempering material, or if the shell is an accidental inclusion due to use of sand from ancient beach deposits.

Incising is by far the commonest decorative technique. Heavy broad-line geometric patterns applied before firing, and usually before slipping, are most frequent. Rows of parallel lines, vertical or horizontal, bands of triangles, hatching and cross-hatching are typical (figs. 82 to 90). More complex patterns sometimes occur (figs. 91–

FIGURES 82–90.—Incised designs, Brown ware and Black ware. Simple geometric designs.

114). Life form are rare, but not absent (figs. 121–131). Post-firing incising runs to fine scratchy geometric patterns, of which the simple cross-hatched triangles (e. g., figs. 86, 87, 88) are typical. Red paint was sometimes rubbed into the incised areas. Modeled relief decoration infrequently occurs (pl. 17), but a fairly constant number

of Brown ware sherds show rude patterns or markings produced by
stick-polishing.

POLISHED BROWN WARE

Polished Brown may be a subvariety of the normal Brown ware,
a variant perhaps intended for ceremonial use. It consists of small

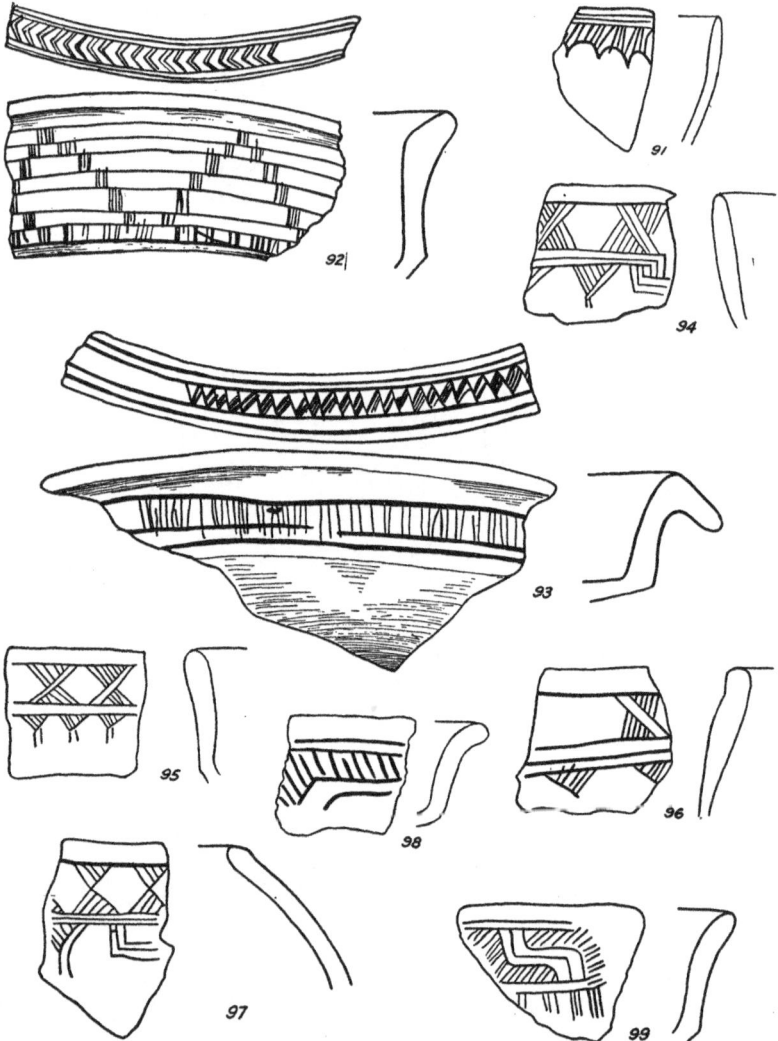

FIGURES 91–99.—Incised designs, Brown ware and Black ware.   Simple to complex geometric
designs.

thin-walled vessels of comparatively elaborate shapes, well-fired, and
with a high gloss.   The slip has about the same color range as normal
Brown ware, but with a higher frequency of olive-brown tones, from

light to dark. The polishing process has left faint streaks on the vessel walls, usually horizontal on the interior and vertical, or vertical over horizontal, on the exterior.

The paste appears to be the same as that of normal Brown ware, being of the same colors, and with the same tempering material. The chief point of difference is that the Polished Brown is much harder, better-fired, and thinner.

As stated, Polished Brown ware shows a tendency to more elaborate forms. Composite-silhouette bowls and small jars are the commonest shapes.

Ordinarily, Polished Brown ware has no other decoration than its glossy surface. A few pieces, however, show traces of paint, usually red, though some black occurs, applied in broad stripes, which must have formed very simple designs.

Incising occurs in rare instances. Most frequent are simple geometric patterns of triangles, etc., applied after firing. Pre-firing incised designs are limited for the most part to broad shallow grooves about the rim and base.

The ware is very like the "Polished Gray ware" of Monte Albán I–II, in which similar finish, vessel shapes, and often even the same olive-brown surface tones appear.

RED WARE

Red ware is essentially a subtype of the local Brown ware, consisting of the same paste, and including many of the vessel forms of the latter. In fact, commonly the red paint is applied over a brown wash.

Red ware is coated all over (except in the case of bowls, in which, as in Brown ware, the bases are frequently left unslipped) with a bright red pigment, apparently micaceous hematite. Often, particularly in specimens from the earlier levels, the pigment is not well fired on, or has deteriorated in the course of time; that of the more recent epochs is harder and glossier. There is little variation in color in well-preserved specimens. The paste is the same as that of Brown ware.

The range of shapes appears not as great as that of Brown ware, chiefly because we have a smaller sampling of complete vessels. Red ware was never very common. It seems probable that, had we a larger quantity of complete specimens, we would find duplicates of most if not all the Brown ware forms.

Red ware is never found with any painted decoration other than its bright-hued slip. Incised decoration is rare, consisting, when it does occur, of small post-firing geometric designs.

RED-ON-BROWN WARE

This ware occurs in three subclasses, two of which, distinguishable at first glance in dealing with whole vessels or even large fragments, are practically impossible to segregate in sorting the run of small sherds from our trenches.

First of all, it is to be noted that both paste and slip of all three subgroups are identical to those of normal Brown ware. There seems to be a tendency toward the dark-olive tones of slip, but the complete range of colors of Brown ware, from bright orange brown to nearly black occurs. On this slip the red paint is applied.

The three subdivisions depend on mode of application of the red pigment. In one, the most common, it is applied in broad horizontal bands, for example about rim and base, or about the middle of the vessel. In the second, it is applied in broad-line patterns (figs. 135, 136, 137). These seem to be for the most part simple combinations of stripes or zigzags. Large dots are occasionally noted. There are no suggestions of elaborate or representative designs. The third subclass is the same as the second, with the addition of post-firing incised lines bordering the red stripes (fig. 138).

NEGATIVE PAINTED WARE

A ceramic group of considerable interest despite its rarity at the site is that with "negative" designs. Nearly all the examples of this ware, if so it may be called, properly belong to the Brown or Red ware groups, being identical in paste and slips, and, wherever determinable, in vessel form as well. Frequently the design elements are formed of the underlying brown slip, with the surrounding areas in red. Less frequently the elements are of a red (ground) color with surrounding areas in a thin black paint. One lone example occurs of a White ware sherd (White-slipped) to which black paint has been applied.

There are too few specimens of Negative Painted ware to generalize about the designs. The best preserved are represented in the accompanying figures 139 and 140. Most seem to be rather simple combinations of lines and dots of varying sizes. There are a few fragments, however, of more elaborate patterns.

BLACK WARE

Black ware forms one of the important ceramic types of Cerro de las Mesas, although never as abundant as Brown ware.

The slip of Black ware appears to be of the same clay as the paste. It is usually moderately well polished, but rarely attains a high gloss.

Off-color examples are not wanting—pieces that are neither quite black nor quite light enough for Brown ware.

The paste used is black in color, with a fairly heavy sand temper. Occasionally small bands or areas show brownish tones instead of black. Many of the vessel forms noted in Brown ware recur in this ceramic group.

Decoration.—The decoration of Black ware is restricted to various types of incising. Painted designs do not occur, unless the red or white paint rubbed into incised patterns be classed as such. Nor are there examples of modeled ornament in the collections. Pre-firing incising is less frequent than that done after the baking process. There seems to be a greater proportion of curvilinear, possibly repre-

FIGURE 100.—Incised design, Black ware.   Complex geometric design.

sentative, designs in this technique. Worth special mention is the broad-line "scraped" decoration of a small number of pieces (pl. 19, *a, e,* and figs. 115–120). The patterns seem to have been applied after drying but before firing, though the practice of rubbing paint into the scraped areas often makes it difficult to be sure at what stage the decorating was done. Post-firing designs are nearly exclusively geometric. Hatched triangles, often flanking parallel lines, appear as one of the most frequent motifs (figs. 82–114).

As mentioned, both red paint and white occur as filler to make the incised designs stand out more sharply. The white pigment is much the rarer of the two.

FIGURES 101–114.—Incised designs, Brown ware and Black ware. Cursive and complex geometric designs.

FIGURES 115–119.—Scraped ("raspada") designs, Brown ware and Black ware.

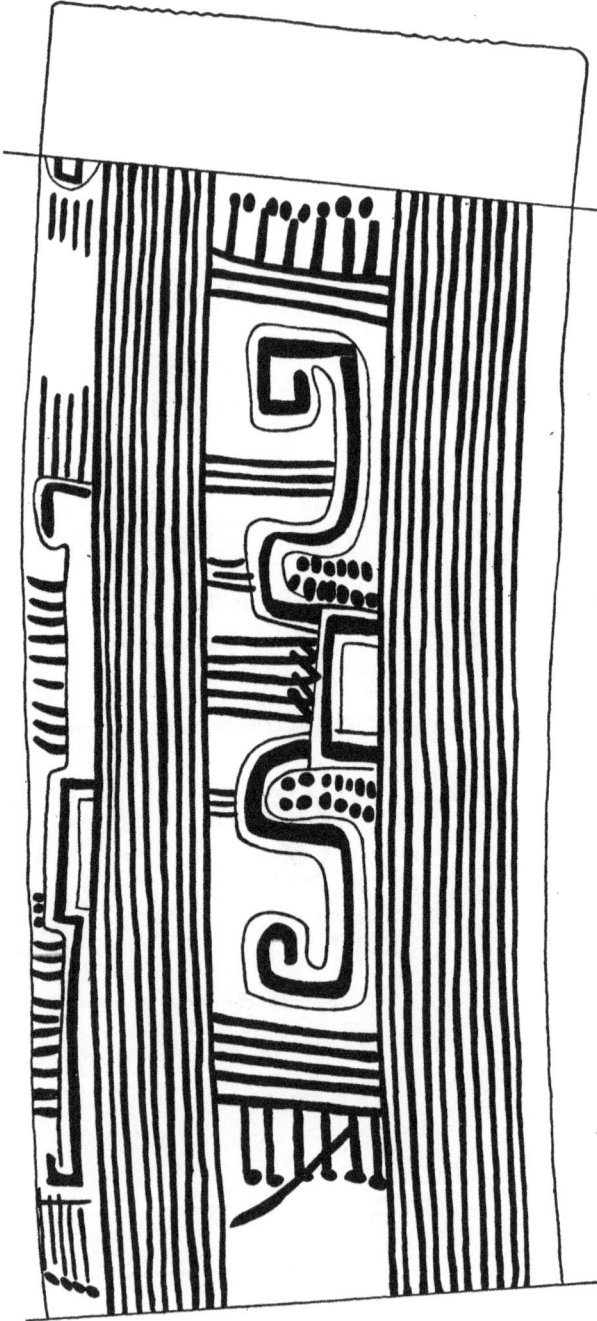

FIGURE 120.—Scraped ("raspada") design, Black ware.

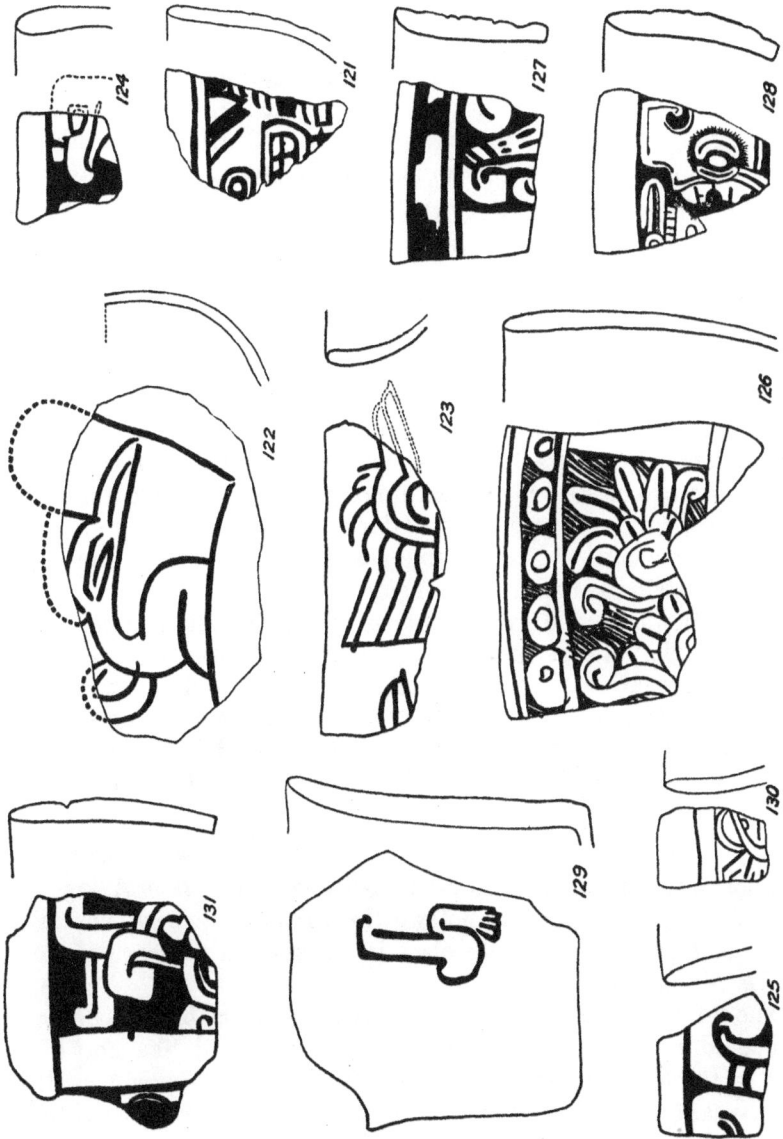

FIGURES 121–131.—Incised representative designs, Brown ware and Black ware.

BLACK-AND-WHITE WARE

Black-and-White is a ware in which, owing to unequal firing, accidental or intended, the slip is in some areas black, in others white. The paste and slip are essentially the same as those of Black ware. This ware, and more especially one of its varieties, is familiar from the Tres Zapotes collections, and has been noted at La Venta.[6] There are two subtypes of the ware, one in which the white portions are irregularly distributed, and the other, more common, in which the white coloring is confined to the rim (pl. 20, c). The latter consists exclusively of flaring straight to convex-side bowls. Decoration consists of the piebald coloring.

WHITE WARE

Sherds of White ware are often difficult to tell apart from white-surfaced fragments of Black-and-White ware. The chief diagnostic is that, in the case of true White ware, the paste differs sharply in color from the slip. Frequently it is gray in color; other examples are a pinkish buff that shows through and gives a warm shade to the slip. This difference in paste color does not warrant separation of the material into two classes, for in texture of paste (porous, medium hard, heavy sand temper), type of slip (thick, glossy), frequency and style of incised decoration, determinable vessel form, and, most important, vertical distribution the two coincide.

Decoration is incised, frequently before slipping and firing. Angular geometric patterns prevail (figs. 132–134). The design elements show close relationship to those of Brown ware and Black ware, in use of hachure, small triangles, and angular S-shaped figures.

Vessel shapes, insofar as they can be determined from the material at hand, consist chiefly of bowls, both of convex and of the straight-side varieties.

MISCELLANEOUS BICHROME WARES

There are, in addition to Red-on-Brown ware, several kinds of Bichrome wares. None is noteworthy in its frequency, but taken together they have a definite place in the vertical sequence of Cerro de las Mesas ceramics.

The pastes of which they are composed are invariably porous, sand-tempered, neither very hard nor very soft; in a word, like most of the rest of the local pastes. In view of the scarcity of specimens, little can be said as to vessel shapes. About all that can be done is to list the several varieties: Red-and-White; White-and-Brown; and Red-on-Cream.

Pre-slip incised examples of Red-and-White are shown in figures 141–142.

---

[6] Stirling, information.

STUCCO PAINTED WARE

A few examples of Stucco Painted ware were recovered in trench 30. The pastes appear similar to those of local ceramics, particularly to that of Brown ware; one sherd is certainly of Black ware. Two complete vessels are similar in form to certain Brown, and Red-on-Brown jars (pl. 21, c, d); two potstands have no counterpart among local restorable forms (pl. 21, a, b). The paints, white, red, green, black, and yellow appear to be of the same material as those of the painted gourd found in trench 19.

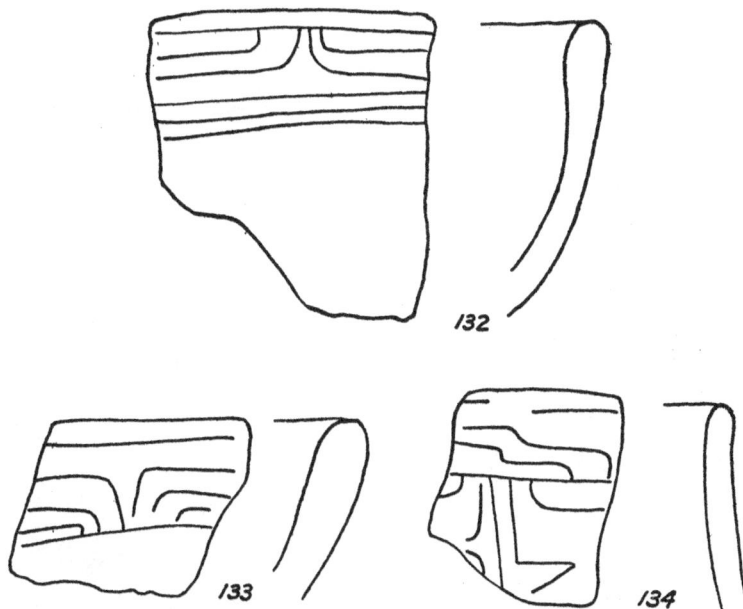

FIGURES 132–134.—Incised designs, White ware.

DULL BUFF POLYCHROME WARE

In contradistinction to the Untempered ware, all the rest of the local Polychromes (there are several varieties) definitely relate to the local Monochrome and Bichrome wares. Some, in fact, are little more than Brown ware vessels to which polychrome designs have been applied.

One of the most abundant of the Cerro de las Mesas Polychrome wares is that designated as "Dull Buff." The paste of this ware is light and porous, buff to brown in color, with sand, and occasionally sand and shell, for tempering material. The slip consists of the same clay, resulting in a surface color dark buff to light brown. While there is some variation, as a rule the surface is but slightly polished.

Directly on this buff wash or slip are applied the designs in red, black, and white paint. In this lack of a prepared base, the ware is

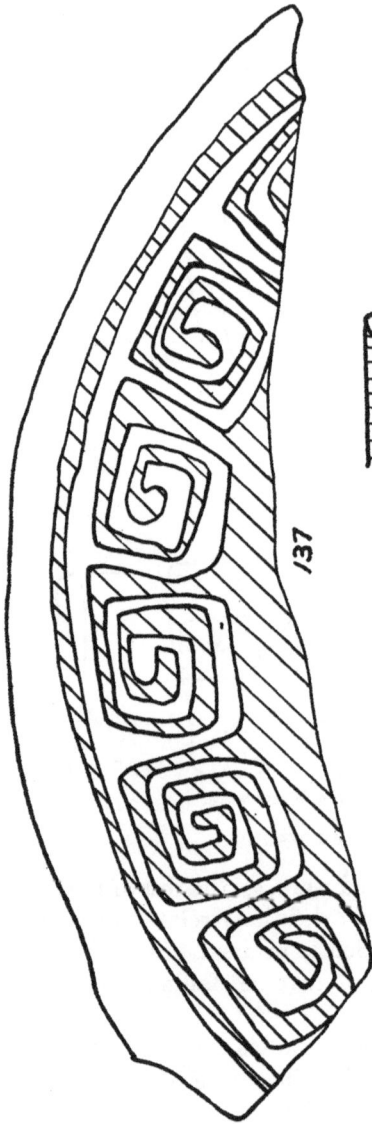

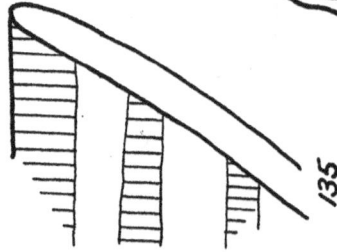

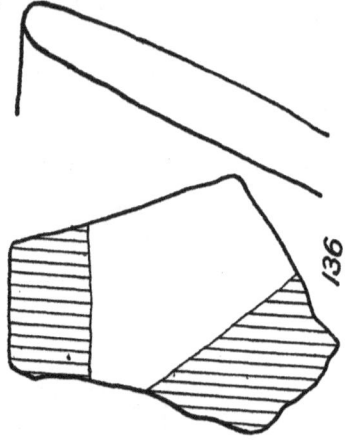

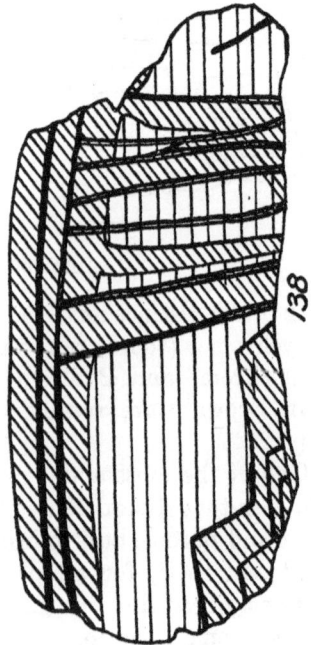

FIGURES 135-138.—Red-on-Brown ware. Hachure (diagonal and vertical) red paint; heavy lines, incising.

very reminiscent of the Black, or Red, on "natural color of the base" wares so characteristic of Cholulteca I and early Aztec horizons. The source of the pigments is not known, but it is noteworthy that the red is not the same micaceous hematite used on Red and Red-on-Brown wares, though nearly the same in color. In fact, in none of the true Polychrome is this material used, at least in recognizable form. Perhaps owing to the nature of the paints, or more likely owing to the lack of surface polish of the slip and the porous nature of the paste, the painted decoration has the same dull finish as the slip. The effect is difficult to describe; one is reminded of the flat

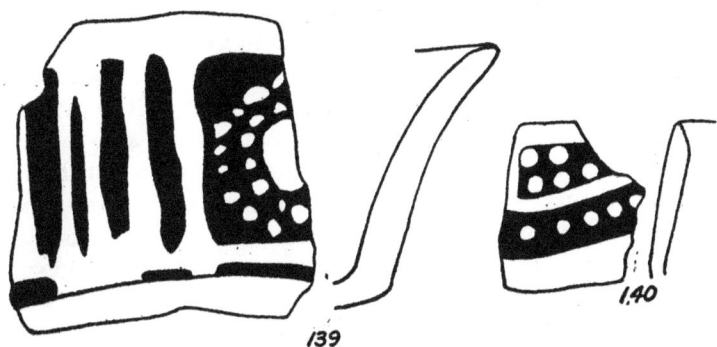

FIGURES 139–140.—Negative Painted ware designs.

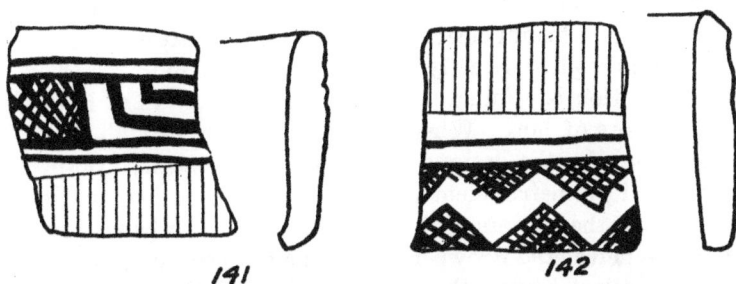

FIGURES 141–142.—Red-and-White Incised ware designs. Vertical hachure, red paint; heavy lines, incising.

lackluster appearance of a priming coat of common house paint on new wood. This very characteristic surface appearance serves to distinguish it almost at a glance from the other Polychromes occurring at the site.

No complete vessels of Dull Buff Polychrome ware have been recovered, but as far as can be told from sherds, the designs are extremely simple, consisting for the most part of broad angular lines arranged in simple geometric patterns. Rows of horizontal lines about the interior rim of bowls is of common occurrence. Broad diagonals descending from the rim, in groups of alternating colors, is likewise frequent. Bold white stripes are sometimes bordered with red or black lines. Infrequently, the interior of a bowl (or possibly a band about the interior) is given a wash of white, on which the linear designs are drawn in black and red. A series of typical design fragments is given in the upper row of plate 1. Their characteristic angularity is as distinctive as the dull tones in which they are painted.

COMPLICATED POLYCHROME WARE

Complicated Polychrome is a ware readily distinguishable from the rest in its use of colors, and mode of application and type of its designs. This ware occurs as an important component of the Cholulteca ceramic complex, where it has been designated "policroma lacá" (Noguera, 1937, p. 3). Since Noguera has not yet described the Cholula ceramics in detail, its major characteristics will be given here. The paste is buff to orange brown, with sand temper, and fairly well fired. Undecorated areas of vessels frequently have a polished light orange brown slip. The colors used are the same as those of Brown Polychrome, red, white, black, and orange, but orange is used much more extensively. The application of the paints to a polished surface produces the "lacquerlike" effect for which the ware was named at Cholula, and results in a characteristic flaking-off of the decorated areas in weathered specimens. Very often the white paint serves also as a slip or foundation for the design. This light base shows through sufficiently to give bright clear tones to the colors, instead of the somber ones of paints applied directly on a dark-hued ground.

The decoration is applied to interiors and exteriors of bowls, and to the exteriors of jars. Where the field is large enough, there is a clear tendency for the designs to be applied in panels. Both representative and geometric elements occur, usually in combination, the latter forming the borders of the decorative panels or bands or serving as filler. Whereas the Brown Polychrome patterns are done in broad none too regular strokes, those of Complicated Polychrome tend to fine, neatly drawn lines, with numerous elements.

Unfortunately, little can be said as to subjects of the representative designs, for sizable well-preserved sherds of the ware are few (cf. pls. 1, 2). A number of fragments have trailing featherlike objects, apparently headdresses or ornaments of elaborately costumed figures. Several sherds show portions of faces and hands. In another case, a row of animal(?) heads forms part of the border of the main design panel.

BROWN POLYCHROME WARE

As the name indicates, this variety of painted ware is the closest of a. to the common Brown ware of the site. In many cases a brown

slip indistinguishable from that of the Monochrome ware forms the
base or background of the designs.   Where some other color serves
this purpose, the underlying brown slip can be seen on unpainted portions such as the bases of bowls.   The paste is the same as that of

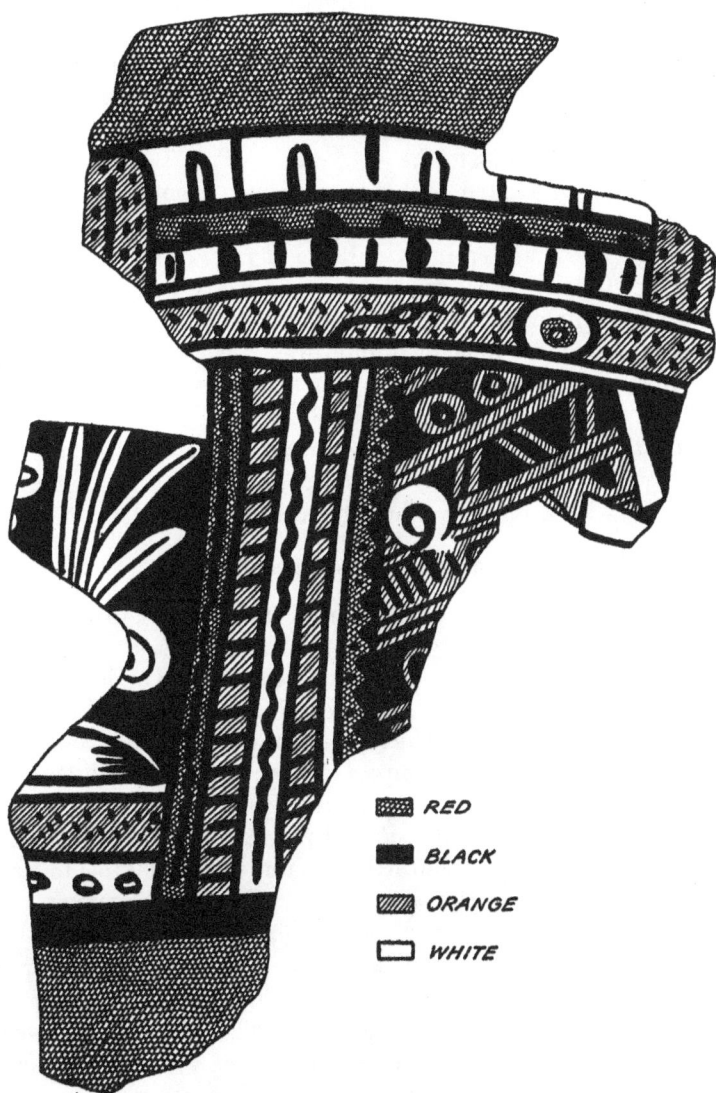

RED
BLACK
ORANGE
WHITE

FIGURE 143.—Complicated Polychrome jar fragment (exterior).

Brown ware, though better fired and thinner (the vessels seem to run
to smaller sizes, as well).   Its surfaces are nearly always well polished.

The colors of the designs are red, black, white, and orange. Orange occurs less frequently than the other colors. The paints contrast sharply with those of Dull Buff ware in their hard glossy surfaces as well as in motifs. Both geometric and representative patterns occur, sometimes in combination; for example, with a representative pattern in the interior of a bowl, and a geometric design about the exterior rim. The representative patterns are boldly painted to the point of cursiveness, usually with black borders about the color areas. As stated, the brown slip commonly serves as the background, but sometimes red paint is used instead.

The motifs, as indicated, are quite variable. Some consist in nothing more complex than pairs of widely spaced vertical black lines with alternating spaces painted in red. Rows of frets or spirals sometimes decorate bowl rims. The representative designs, owing to their extreme conventionalization and, as well, the cursive manner in which they were painted, are difficult to interpret. The series of figures will convey a better impression of them than many paragraphs of text (pl. 1; fig. 144). Sometimes bowl interiors are painted solid red, with the design on the exterior only. A specialized bowl type of this ware, equipped with a molded interior bottom (pl. 53, *m* to *q*) is normally painted only with a few broad horizontal lines about the rim.

BLACK-AND-WHITE-ON-RED WARE

Black-and-White-on-Red ware, along with a Black-on-Red variant, occurs with the Brown Polychrome, and at first was regarded as a subvariety of the latter, since paste and vessel forms and, as well, the brown slip underlying the red background color indicate close technological relationship. That is to say, even though the Black-and-White-on-Red pattern was probably imported from the Highland, if we may judge by its frequency there on relatively late horizons (Noguera, 1935, pp. 151, 179, et passim.), it was promptly hybridized with the local Brown Polychrome. Nevertheless, it seems preferable to set this ceramic group, or subgroup, as one may wish to designate it, off by itself to call attention to a very clear Highland relationship.

Both the black and the red paints used were full-bodied paints permitting a high polish. The white paint, on the other hand, is fugitive. An attempt was made to distinguish between two variants of the ware according to presence or absence of white paint, but this is probably not very significant, for some sherds counted as Black-on-Red may have actually had parts of their designs in white originally.

BLACK-ON-RED INCISED WARE

This ceramic group is closely related to the Black-and-White-on-Red ware, and through this to Brown Polychrome, but is given separate status because of the different decorative technique. The paste and underlying brown slip are the same. Over the slip is a coat of red

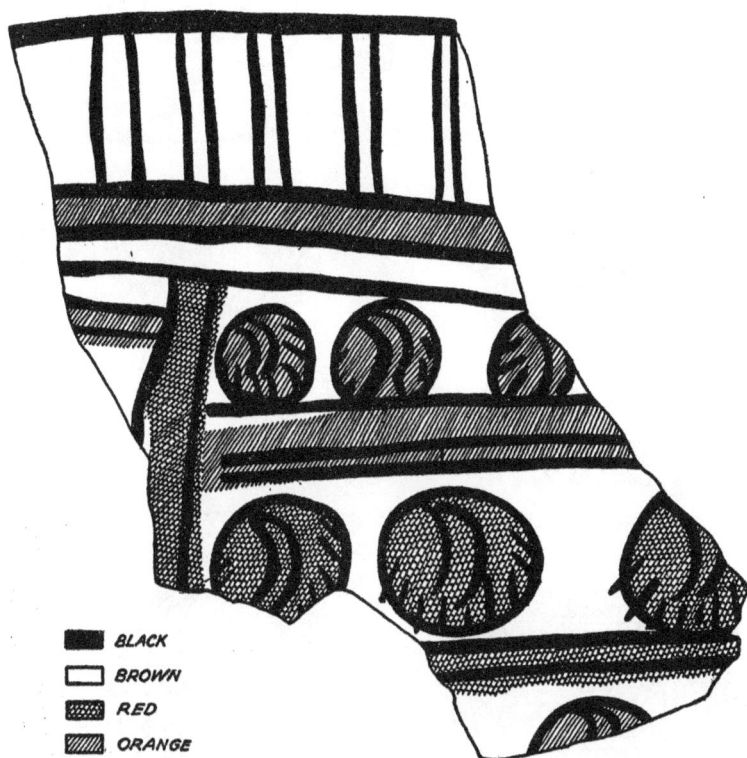

BLACK
BROWN
RED
ORANGE

FIGURE 144.—Brown Polychrome jar fragment (exterior).

paint, usually in a broad band about the exterior sides of bowls. There are two subtypes of the ware, depending on the variety of decoration. In one, broad stripes of black contain small geometric post-firing incised designs (fig. 145). Spirals, circles, frets, etc., are common elements. In the other variety, the black paint forms the design, usually more elaborate, and is outlined or accentuated by post-firing incising (figs. 143, 144, 146 to 149). One of the few nearly complete vessels of this kind bears essentially the same designs as a Black-and-White-on-Red bowl (cf. figs. 149 and 150). This ware is well known from Cerro Montoso, as well as from Cholulteca horizons, and Aztec levels of the valley.

RED   BLACK   WHITE   ORANGE

FIGURE 145.—Black-and-White-on-Red bowl fragment (interior).

147

146

149

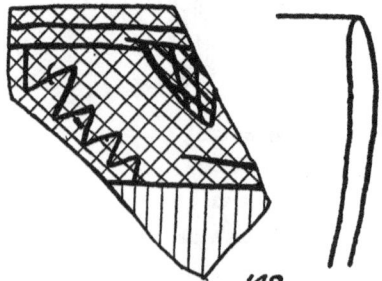

148

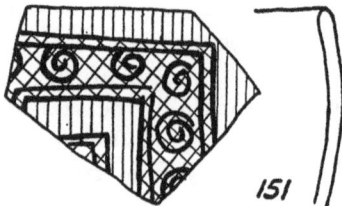

151

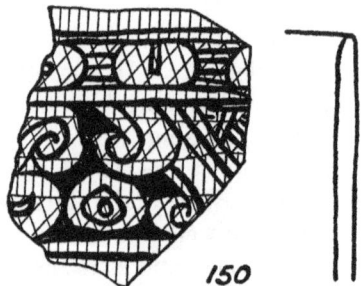

150

FIGURES 146–151.—Black-on-Red Incised ware designs. Vertical hachure, red; cross hachure, black; heavy lines, incising.

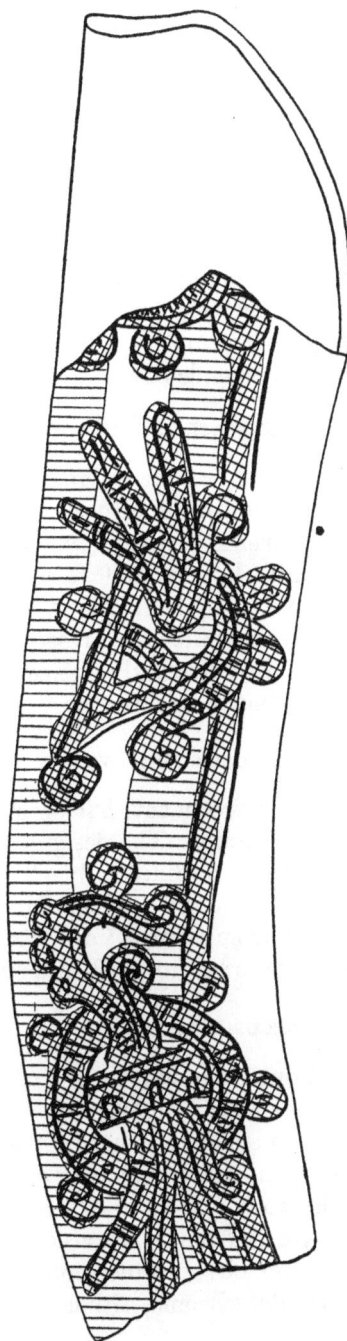

FIGURE 152.—Black-on-Red Incised ware.   Vertical hachure, red; cross hachure, black; heavy lines, incising.

RED-ON-ORANGE INCISED WARE

Red-on-Orange Incised can be classed as a Polychrome only if we count the basic paste color that shows in the incised areas as a separate tone. However, due to the similarity to the Black-on-Red Incised ware, and since, moreover, its vertical distribution can be shown to coincide with that of the true Polychromes, the ware will be included with that major ceramic division.

The paste is similar to that of Brown Polychrome; the slip is orange brown. Nearly always three to five narrow lines of red run about the interior rim, and broad stripes, which contain the postfiring incised decorative elements, run about the exterior. Circles, spirals, etc., are the commonest motifs. The only identifiable vessel form is that of the open convex-side bowl.

FINE-LINE BLACK-ON-WHITE WARE

This is a ware of infrequent occurrence, found only in late mounds of the site. It may be a trade ware, although in paste and pigment it resembles Brown Polychrome very closely. It is characterized by use of large areas of white background (over a light-brown slip) with precise neatly drawn designs in black. Both geometric and what appear to be conventionalized representative patterns occur (pl. 4, c–f). Red paint is used sparingly adjacent to the main design areas. Open convex-side bowls are the only form known in this ware.

TAN POLYCHROME WARE

Another ware of very low frequency, but of interest for comparative purposes, is Tan Polychrome. The designs are applied over the light-buff slip in white and red, outlined in black (pl. 4, a, b). In the Museo Nacional de Mexico there are very similar specimens from the Isla de los Sacrificios [7] and from central Veracruz. This ware, or one form of it, is sometimes referred to as White-on-Cream ware (Noguera, 1937).

MISCELLANEOUS POLYCHROME ELEMENTS

Included in the collections are a number of examples of zoomorphic vessel legs, and cylindrical loop handles with zoomorphic ornament that undoubtedly belong to one or another of the Polychrome wares, but in the absence of more nearly complete specimens it is difficult to assign them to a specific ware (pl. 53, a–l). Slips vary from red to orange brown; some have the modeling accentuated by post-firing incised designs. This latter circumstance conflicts with their determination as Complicated Polychrome, although zoomorphic legs and

---

[7] See also Nuttall, 1910, passim., and Novelo, 1928, ftn. 16, p. 61.

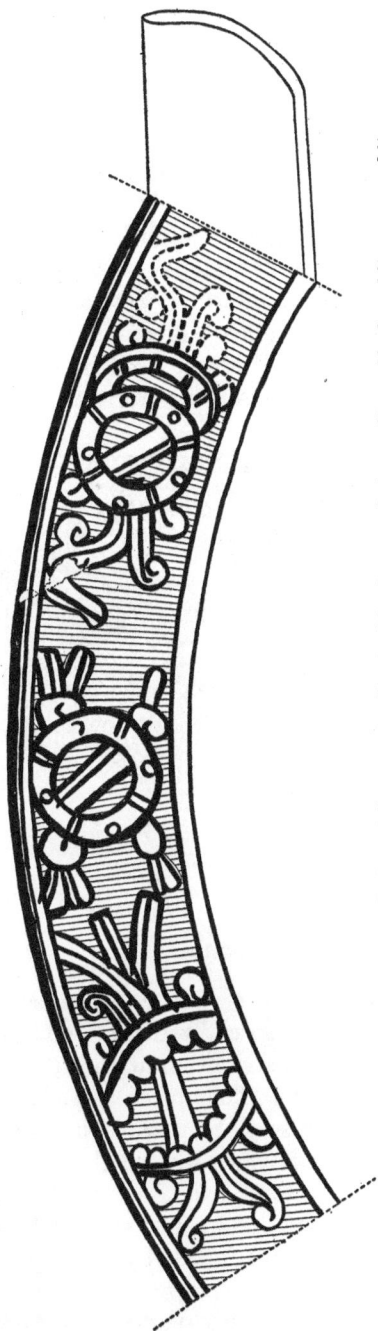

FIGURE 153.—Black-and-White-on-Red bowl (exterior). Vertical hachure, red; heavy lines, black; white areas, white.

appendages occur in this ware at Cholula. It may be that they occurred in both Complicated and Brown Polychrome, and even perhaps in the Incised wares closely related to the latter.

COARSE RED-RIMMED BOWLS

There are in the collections numerous sherds and a number of complete examples of a type of unpolished, unslipped shallow bowl, of buff sandy paste, 10 to 16 inches in diameter, and 3 to 4 inches deep. Rims vary from simple to slightly thickened. Most of these bowls have a broad stripe of red paint about the rim; a few have similar stripes across to the interior. Several were found serving as covers for burial pots or ollas. A number of fragments contain quantities of the burned shell stucco used in structures—possibly an important function of the vessels was for mixing this material.

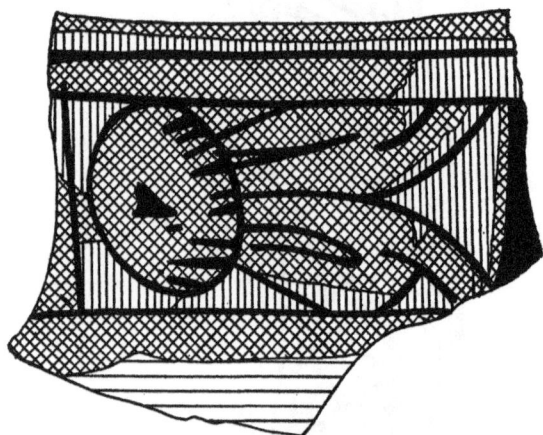

FIGURE 154.—Black-and-White-on-Red ware fragment. Vertical hachure, red; cross hachure, black; heavy lines, white.

COMALES

Comales could perhaps be classed as a variety of Brown ware. In view, however, of their specialized form and function, and their sharply definable vertical distribution at the site, it seems preferable to give them separate status. The objects are of a hard brown to buff paste, with fairly heavy sand temper. The rim and interior are coated with a well-polished brown slip which has the same color range as that of Brown ware, although tending to the darker olive-brown shades (orange browns, etc., occur, but are not common). The base of the utensil is not only unslipped, but is apparently deliberately roughened. The vessels range from 12 to 18 or 20 inches in diameter, and are gently concave, probably varying between 2 and 5 inches

in depth. The rims are thickened on the exterior (or under) side.
Rim sherds with small triangular tabs occur, but in the absence of
complete vessels it is impossible to state whether or not these were
a standard feature, or how many there were to each comal.

MONUMENTAL WARE

This is a ware which in one sense bridges the gap between vessels
and figurines, for it includes both vessellike objects and figures of men,
beasts, or gods. For convenience in the field, and because of certain resemblances to the large incensarios of nearby regions, we referred to this class of objects as "Incensario ware," but there is no
evidence that they actually had such a function. More likely correct
is a suggestion made by Stirling, that the vessellike objects in this ware
were stands or pedestals for the idols made of the same type of clay.
The fact that nearly all the examples collected were found in mounds,
not in the refuse deposits, supports one opinion no more than the
other.

The paste used is coarse, porous, and sandy, varying from medium
to soft in hardness. It is never more than smoothed on the surface,
at times being quite rough. A coarse white paint, which appears to
be a wash of the stucco used for structures, was often applied. Less
frequently a red paint was used. Some specimens show no trace of
paint of any kind. A number appear to have been in the form of
rectangular boxes, 8 inches to 1 foot high, about the same in width,
and over 2 feet long; others were round (pl. 8, c, d).

The exteriors were decorated in a variety of ways. Large closely
set bosses are common. Strips of appliqué form designs, some simple
geometric patterns, others representative. One example (trench 34)
was decorated with the grim features of a Tlaloc. It may be that
such objects as the jaguar head (pl. 45, e) were affixed to the sides
of these pedestals. Rectangular or T-shaped perforations, cut
through while the clay was soft, sometimes occur.

Of the same paste, finish, and type of paint as these pedestals, and
decorated in part in the same appliqué technique, are certain large
figures, or idols. The heads of two types of these are often of more
than human size (pls. 44, 45, 47), and the fragments of bodies, limbs,
etc., associated with them indicate that the complete figures must
have been proportionately large. The features are free-modeled, with,
as already stated, appendages of appliqué. Some fragments from
trench 34 are nearly 1½ inches in thickness. The artistry of these
idols far surpasses that of the large figures from the Highland, such
as that recovered by Linné from a Mazapan horizon.

Plain ware consists chiefly of large ollas, though there are a few cache or offertory jars that may be included in this classification. The paste is porous with a heavy sand temper, and varies from medium soft to fairly well fired. In form the ollas are round-bodied, with well-defined neck joints and ordinarily, flaring necks (pl. 25, *a*, figs. 62 to 72). Three types of bases occur: round, flattened, and low annular ring. The rounded and the flattened bases are most common. There does not appear to be any sharp correlation between any one type of base and neck.

A few flat-based cylindrical-walled jars of Plain ware were found in mound excavations (pl. 25, *b*, *c*, *d*). Several contained collections of marine shells. These vessels were invariably poorly fired, to the point of crumbling on exposure and the consequent drying out of the paste. They were probably made, in haste or carelessly, for the express purpose of burying in the mounds; their crudity and softness would prevent their serving any utilitarian end.

Included in the collections are several specimens that resemble certain forms from Teotihuacán and Tres Zapotes. These are heavy hollow cylindrical handles or lugs, blunt-ended, with perforations or rude modeling to suggest features. Portions of rims attached to them indicate that they rose vertically or slightly inclined inward from the broad flaring rims of rough Plain ware vessels. No restorable vessels of this type were found, however, so that it is not possible to state whether they were of the flat-based slightly flaring-side form known from Teotihuacán, or of the convex side variety found at Tres Zapotes. The lugs themselves are cruder and less elaborately modeled than at either of these sites (pl. 55, 24″–36″). (See stratigraphic material from 24- to 36-inch level, trench 13, on pl. 55.)

Carved ware, in the sense of a distinct ceramic type, does not occur at Cerro de las Mesas. Occasional sherds are found, however, with carved decorations. These belong to various local wares—Brown, Black, etc. One rather elaborately carved fragment is of Red-on-Brown ware (fig. 131). None of the designs are complete, but the better-preserved fragments suggest that they consisted of rather elaborately carved figures (figs. 121, 127, 131).

PLUMBATE WARE

The only example of Plumbate was the complete whistling jar found in trench 15, under conditions that make its temporal relation to the local ceramic column difficult (pl. 10, *d*). The similarity of this specimen to a whistling jar from Honduras is remarkable (cf. pl. 23, and Saville, 1916, pl. 2). Whistling jars, of course, have a wide distribution in the Mexican Highland, occurring in the Mixteca (of Puebla and of Oaxaca), in Teotihuacán, and in the Tarascan area (Noguera, 1937 a, p. 17 *ff*.).

FINE ORANGE WARE

No sherds certainly identifiable as Fine Orange were recovered. The possible relationship of this ware to the Untempered wares of southern and central Veracruz has been mentioned elsewhere (p. 34).

SIEVES

A few sherds of small vessels with perforations made close together while the clay was still soft have been recovered from cuts in mounds assignable to the latest horizon of the site. These are probably importations; they occur too rarely to be considered a local type.

VESSEL SHAPES

To simplify the discussion of vessel forms occurring in the various Cerro de las Mesas wares, and at the same time to save needless repetition, the complete range of shapes represented in the collections will be presented and followed by their distribution among the several wares. It will be noted that there is a very definite trend toward community of forms in the Monochrome and Bichrome wares; that is to say, while the same forms are not represented in all the wares, there is considerable overlap. Brown ware, being most abundant, shows the greatest range of shapes, nearly all of which recur, however, in one or another of its companion wares. Were our sample of the latter fuller, the cooccurrences would undoubtedly be more numerous. There are relatively few restorable examples of Polychrome vessels, so that our list is unduly short as regards these wares. The more common shapes occur in these Polychrome wares, however, suggesting that in a general way they, too, conform. As elsewhere stated, Untempered ware shows the greatest divergence from the local shape patterns, being in this respect, as in paste and slip type, distinct.

The key letters in the following descriptions refer to the accompanying scale drawings (fig. 12). It is to be understood that vessel bases are flat and rims of the simple direct type, unless otherwise indicated.

DESCRIPTION OF VESSEL SHAPES SHOWN IN FIGURE 12

Bowls and dishes

Key

a, a'. Shallow bowls and dishes, flaring convex sides.
   b. Deep bowls, flaring convex sides.
   c. Deep bowls, flaring convex sides, slightly returned.
   d. Shallow bowls and dishes, flaring convex sides, flat everted rim.
   e. Shallow bowls, round bases, flaring convex sides, tripod supports.
   e'. Shallow bowls, rounded bases with central concavity.
f, f'. Deep bowls, incurved sides.
   g. Deep bowls, incurved sides, everted rim, bases?
   h. Deep bowls, incurved returned sides.
i, i'. Same as *h*, but with point of return of sides accentuated to angle, body frequently fluted.
j, j'. Shallow bowls and dishes, flaring straight to concave sides.
   j''. Same as *j, j'*, but with everted rim.
k, k', k''. Same as *j, j'*, with tripod supports (*k*, hollow slab legs; *k'*, hollow hemispherical feet; *k''*, hollow subconical legs).
   l. Deep bowls, flaring straight to concave sides.
m, m'. Shallow composite silhouette bowls and dishes.
   n. Same as *m, m'*, with everted, often down-turned rim.
   n'. Same as *m, m'*, with low annular base.
   o. Deep composite silhouette bowls.
p, p'. Composite silhouette bowls and dishes with angle accentuated to flange.
   q. Large deep-bodied composite silhouette bowls.

Jars and vases

   r. Slightly flaring concave sides.
   r'. Same as *r*, with flaring rim; some had horizontally placed small handles.
s, s'. Same as *r*, with tripod supports; often with incised or appliqué ornament about base.
   t. Vertical to slightly convex sides, bulbous base.
   u. Flaring concave sides, bulbous base, tall annular support.
   v. Same as *u*, but with tripod supports.
   v'. Same as *v*, with bulbous base modified to flange (some *v* and *v'* forms have flaring to everted rims).
   w. Tall annular base, probably pear-shaped bodies.
   w'. Tall annular base, angle at joint of base and body, tall slender tapering body.

Spouted vessels

   x. Low bulbous base, tall slender sides (or neck), flaring rim, supported spout attached to rim.
   y. Wide-mouthed vessels, flaring to everted rim, supported spout attached to neck or body, body ample, probably nearly globular.
   z. Low squat open-spout vessels, probably with vertical handles.
   z'. Tall open-spout pitchers, vertical handles cylindrical in cross section.

Ollas

aa, aa', aa''. Vertical to flaring necks, short to tall, bodies approaching spherical, various types of base (*aa*, leveled; *aa'*, flat; *aa''*, round).

bb. Neckless, rounded to flat base, two (?) flat semicircular lugs.

cc. Low annular bases.

Miscellaneous

dd. Comales; thickened rim, shallow concave body; upper surface polished, lower rough.

ee. "Frying pan" incensarios; hollow cylindrical handle, occasionally terminated in modeled ornament.

ff. (Small) effigy vessels.

gg. Potstands.

hh. "Ladles"; asymmetric, oval in outline.

TABLE 4.—Distribution of vessel shapes (see fig. 12)

Wares	Bowls and dishes																	Jars and vases							Spouted vessels			Ollas			Miscellaneous			
	a	b	c	d	e	f	g	h	i	f	k	l	m	n	o	p	q	r	s	t	u	v	w	w'	x	y	z	aa	bb	cc	dd	ee	ff	gg
Dull Buff Polychrome		×	×							×	×													×			×							
Brown Polychrome		×								×								×																
Complicated Polychrome	×	×	×			×	×																											
Black-and-White-on-Red		×								×																	×							
Black-on-Red Incised		×																																
Red-on-Orange Incised		×		×						×													×			×	×							
Untempered ware																															×			
Comales																																		
Coarse Red-rim bowls		×																								?		×						
Brown ware		×																							?									
Polished Brown ware	×																											×				×		×
Red-on-Brown ware																												×						
Red ware	×	×				×	×	×	×	×	×		×	×		×	×	×	×		×	×			?			×				×		×
Black ware		×			×	×	×	×	×	×	×	×	×		×	×		×	×	×	×	×							×	×			×	
Black-and-White ware		×				×		×		×	×	×	×		×	?				×		×						×						
White ware		×				×		×	×	×		×			×			×		×		×												
Plain ware								×		×		×						×		×														
Stuccoed ware								×		×		×																				×		
Negative Painted ware										×		×							×													×		×

FIGURINES

The figurine collections of the expedition are varied in origin, coming from stratitrench tests, from mound cuts, and, as well, in purchase lots. As luck would have it, some of the most complete and artistically the finest specimens came from the last-mentioned category, and can be placed chronologically only by comparison with unhandsome fragments from the controlled excavations. Enough identifiable scraps occurred in the stratigraphic sections, however, to enable us to establish a sequence of types, as will be demonstrated presently.

Classification of the figurines is based on both technique and style. Hand-made, mold-made, and free modeled are readily distinguishable. Within each of these technologic groups are divisions based on form which have been considered typologic units. The empiric proof that these "types" represent unit cultural complexes rests, of course, on their significant distribution. Subtypes can be, and in cases where number of specimens warrants, have been defined, but do not serve for stratigraphic analyses, because of the small number and fragmentary nature of the material.

There are three figurine types which occur in sufficient quantity to be considered proper to the ceramic pattern under consideration; these are the first three, with their several subtypes, of the following list. In addition, there occur some half a dozen other types which may have been made locally, but which, by their relative scarcity, must be considered imitations of alien forms. The obvious trade pieces, few in number and unquestionable as to source, are not included in the present typology. They are dealt with elsewhere. The final type, the large idols, although a local and relatively frequently occurring form, are left till last because they have already been mentioned under the head of "Monumental Ware." The types are as follows:

I. Hand-made punctate figurines (variants of Tres Zapotes hand-made figurine pattern).
   A. Tres Zapotes subtype A, and variants (pl. 27, *a–j*).
   D. Tres Zapotes type D, and variants (pls. 27, *k, l;* 50, *a*).
   G. Long conical heads with hair sometimes indicated by punctations; eyes, mouth, formed by single horizontal or in-slanting heavy grooves, sometimes in appliqué pellets of clay; ears, earplugs, indicated by punctations. Bodies heavy, nearly shapeless, solid or hollow, with stumpy arms and legs. Figurines frequently painted red or black. Many of small examples have lateral hole through head for suspension. Paste coarse, heavy sand temper. Size: 2¼ in. to approx. 5 in. (pls. 27, *m–s;* 50, *a;* 52).
   H. Eyes vary from Tres Zapotes pattern in consisting of appliqué pieces; the typical horizontal groove and central dot have been punched. Large prominent noses suggest Tres Zapotes type B. Mouth is appliqué piece of clay with 4 or 5 punctations giving the effect of teeth. Ears and/or ear plugs punctate. Headdresses sometimes elaborate, with punctations or grooves. Bodies wide,

flat, with stumpy arms and legs; breasts, navels, sometimes indicated by punctations (pl. 27, u–cc).

X. This designation has been assigned to animal forms manufactured in the same technique, and of the same paste as the foregoing, but which because of variable subject matter are less amenable to classification (pl. 28).

II. Small flat mold-made type.

Small (3¼ in. to 8 in. high; average about 5 in.); broad flat faces with features in low relief, sometimes slightly retouched (noses often added or accentuated after molding). Eyes indicated with brows, lids, and eyeballs in relief; mouth slightly open (teeth *not* indicated). Back of head flat to concave, from pressing into mold. Bodies normally flat, slightly angular, usually standing, although seated forms occur (pls. 30, 31, 33). Feet protrude enough to maintain figurines erect. Arms at sides or across abdomen, in low relief, with hands very sketchily indicated. A small proportion of specimens in the collections have heads belonging to this type stuck on to crude cylindrical bodies with appliqué arms and legs (pl. 32). Figures usually dressed, with tunic, or loose shirt and skirt; some have belts and breechclouts. Necklaces frequently represented. Breasts fairly often represented. Back of body slightly concave. Frequent traces of coats of white "stucco" paint. This type, it may be noted in passing, occurs commonly at Cholula.

A. Most common subvariety distinguished by stylized, rather pleasing faces, all of which are remarkably similar (pl. 29). Headdresses range from thin turbans to less common elaborate forms.

B. A small group of figurines of this type apparently represent dead individuals, with drooping eyelids and sagging mouths. Sometimes the tongue protrudes slightly (pl. 33).

C. Another small group represent monkey beings, with protuberant foreheads, round eyes, and marked prognathism (pl. 35).

D. Sunken-cheeked old men, with prominent noses and marked prognathism, form another subvariety. Variant subforms, represented by a few specimens each, include Tlalocs, Death's Heads (pls. 24, 34), and various animals and birds (pls. 36, 37, 38).

III. Large flat mold-made type.

Typical specimen 10 in. long by 6 in. wide by ½ in. thick. Features, except nose, in very low relief. Tall headdress, bifurcated. Bodies quite angular; arms, hands, feet, dress, crudely indicated (pl. 39). Backs of figurines quite flat. The variation in this type is extremely slight; no subtypes can be segregated.

The following types are represented in our collections by but few specimens only:

IV. A. Rancho de las Animas type (pl. 40, a–i). These figurines seem to be derived, or slightly modified forms. Their characteristics are as follows: Hand-made, with considerable use of appliqué; of well-fired gritty dark-brown paste. Faces are flat, triangular, with horizontal slits for eyes, large appliqué blobs of clay for nose and mouth, appliqué headdresses, earplugs, etc. Bodies hand-made, usually solid (except in case of whistles), stubby limbs, often a tripod to stand erect. Clothing (ornaments, capes, skirts) appliquéd on. Asphalt paint frequent.

B. A variant type, possibly a hybrid of IV–A and type I. The heads approach
type I in form and cylindrical cross section; features are indicated as
in IV–A (pl. 40, *j–m*).

V. A type closely related to the preceding but with modeled features: brows,
eyelids, noses, etc. (pl. 40, *n, o*). Faces may be mold-made. Headdresses, ornaments, clothing, appliquéd. One specimen of this type is represented lying in a cot (or cradle?). This is undoubtedly a hybrid type.
Open mouths with prominent incisors of the Laughing Face type occur in
some specimens.

VI. Open-backed mold-made type (pl. 41, *a–c*, fig. 155). This is a form
probably proper to Central Veracruz, although its center of distribution
has not been defined as yet. Principally human representations, made in
deep mold, edges finished off smooth. Most or all equipped with short-
stemmed whistle stuck on in middle of back. (See fig. 155.) Figures
rather simple, without much ornamentation, faces wide, moderate low-
relief features, frequently with opened mouth reminiscent of Laughing
Face type. Clay gritty, well-fired, polished; Brown slip most common.
Painted decoration, most often in red.[8]

VII. San Marcos mold-made type.

A very few examples of the elaborate mold-made type of figurines
distinctive of the Upper Tres Zapotes period occur in the collections
(pl. 41, *d–h*). Fortunately, enough of these have been found in
deposits of known position, in the Cerro de las Mesas ceramic series,
to make them useful for cross-dating.

VIII. Laughing Face type.

A. This category is reserved for the classic Laughing Face figurines,
large (8 to 10 in. tall), with sloping forehead, high triangular headdress, open "laughing" mouth with prominent incisors. Bodies
hollow, often infantile in proportions; hands often raised to sides
of head open or grasping hanks of hair. Sometimes nude; when
clothed, elaborate geometric designs applied in relief to garments.
This type is actually extremely rare at the site of Cerro de las Mesas,
although the collections include some specimens from nearby localities (pl. 42, *a, b*).

B. Small variants of A (pl. 42, *c–m*). This group, distinctively small
in comparison to the classic variety, is of more frequent occurrence
at our site. Some present all the elements of the classic type save
size; others retain but few. There are as well specimens patently
hybrid in form, combining features of VIII–B with those of other
figurine types, which are often difficult to distinguish. Typologically VIII–B figurines could be either ancestral to or derived from
the classic type (VIII–A).

IX. Masks and maskettes (pl. 43).

A group of objects apparently mold-made, and retouched, with perforations at the upper corners for suspension. The faces are triangular
in form, with concave backs and finished edges. Sometimes there
are holes at eyes and mouth. Some appear to be Xipe-representa-
tions, with half-closed eyes and open mouth. Others display
jaguarlike fangs, and occasionally elaborate nose ornaments.

---

[8] Two figurines of this type were encountered at Tres Zapotes in an Upper period deposit
in 1940.

X. Large free-modeled idols.

These are the clay figures that belong to the Monumental ware previously described. They tend to be quite large, free-modeled, with appliqué ornaments (pls. 45–48). In paste type, firing, surface finish, painting, etc., they correspond to the vessels and pedestals associated with them. Too few complete examples have been recovered to warrant classification into subtypes. Large tubular arms and legs, often with realistically modeled hands and feet, apparently belong to these figures. In technique and finish the objects of this class suggest the (smaller) Lirios type figurines of Upper Tres Zapotes, and as well the figurine material reported on by Weyerstall from the Tesechoacan.

MINOR OBJECTS OF CLAY

In addition to vessels and figurines, there are a number of minor types of objects of baked clay, some of which are important strati-

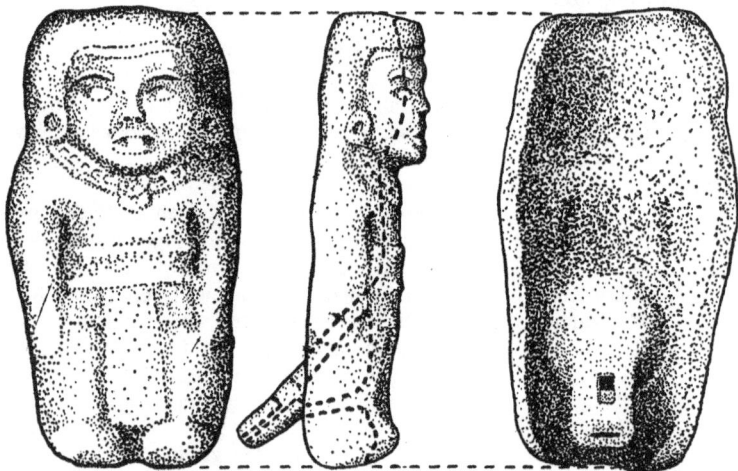

FIGURE 155.—Figurine type VI. Front, side, and back views.

graphically. Among these are spindle whorls, flutes, clay pellets, seals, and large tubes.

The spindle whorls (figs. 170–199) (perforated sherd disks are not included here) are varied in form but can be divided into several groups: Plain (including flat, hemispherical, conical, etc., in profile); elaborate silhouette; and those with modeled ornament. Those of the first type are frequently painted black or red, or with simple designs in black on red. Those with modeled ornament frequently are coated with a black pigment which appears to be asphaltum.

The clay flutes are usually red painted. No complete examples occur in the collections, but several pieces appear to have been of 4-holed instruments. The distal ends are open and surmounted by modeled ornaments—heads of men or animals, hands, feet, flowers, etc. (figs. 156–169).

The clay pellets are roughly globular, ranging from ¼ to ⅝ of an inch in diameter. They are hand-made, not molded. Almost invariably, they are painted red or black; a few have a coat of dark-brown paint. The function of the objects is uncertain. They are not "sounders" for vessel supports, for the latter are not painted. Their

FIGURES 156–169.—Flutes with modeled ornament.

irregularity of size makes use in pellet blowguns, or similar arms, unlikely, and they are too small to be effective ammunition for slings (except possibly for small birds). They might be gaming pieces, counters, or sounders for rattles.

Seals are relatively rare at Cerro de las Mesas. None were found in the stratigraphic trenches. Both the flat and the cylindrical varieties occur in the collections, mostly from lots of purchased material. A series of designs are shown in figures 200–208.

Large cylinders of coarse, unpainted ware 1 foot 8 inches to 2 feet long, and 7 to 9 inches in diameter, were found laid in lines like modern

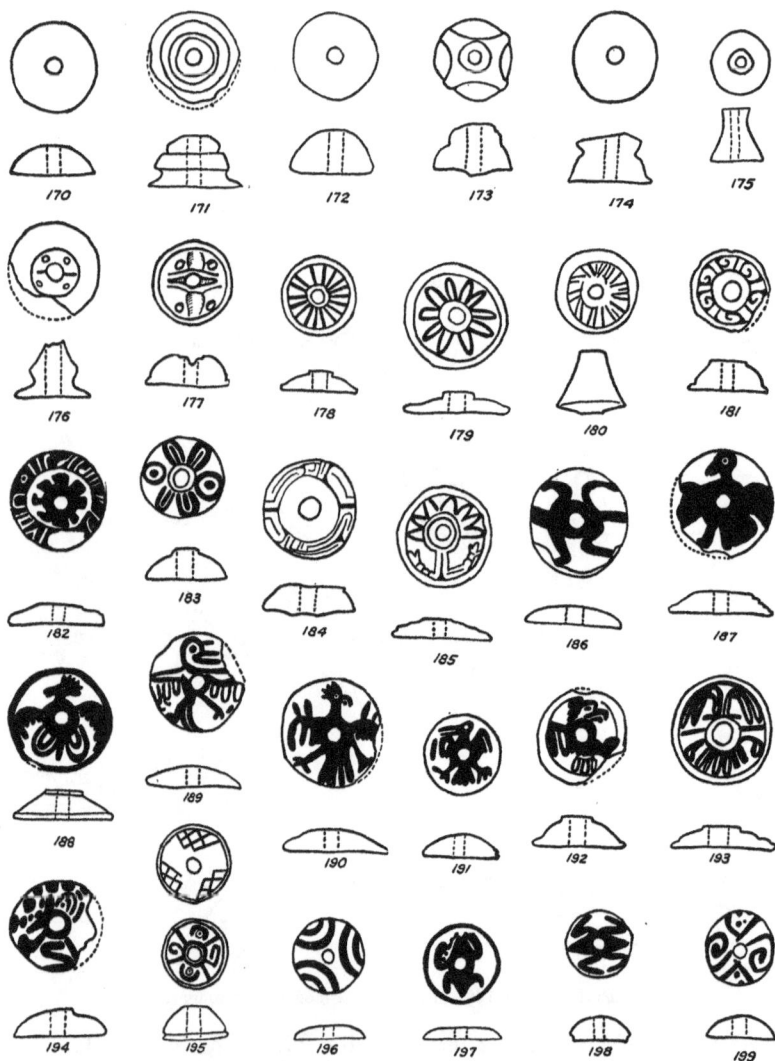

FIGURES 170–199.—Spindle whorls. Figures 170–172, 174–175, plain; figures 176–195, relief (molded) ornament; figures 196–199, painted ornament.

sewer pipes, with the ends telescoped, in two mounds in the Small Mound Locality. Their function was more likely ritual than utilitarian. One example of such a "pipe line" was found at the Ranchito locality at Tres Zapotes, and they also occur in connection with Zapote-can tombs.

Small double rings of clay, usually of Brown or Black ware, with the planes of the loops at right angles, occur in the deposits. Their function is unknown, but they have a sharply delimited vertical distribution.

FIGURES 200–208.—Designs from seals.

STRATIGRAPHY

WARE DISTRIBUTIONS

The vertical distributions of wares and miscellaneous ceramic types will be treated under a series of heads: first the wares, then special features of form, and finally figurines and miscellaneous objects of clay. It is necessary to make the separation between the ware counts and the formal features, because the latter represent in many cases

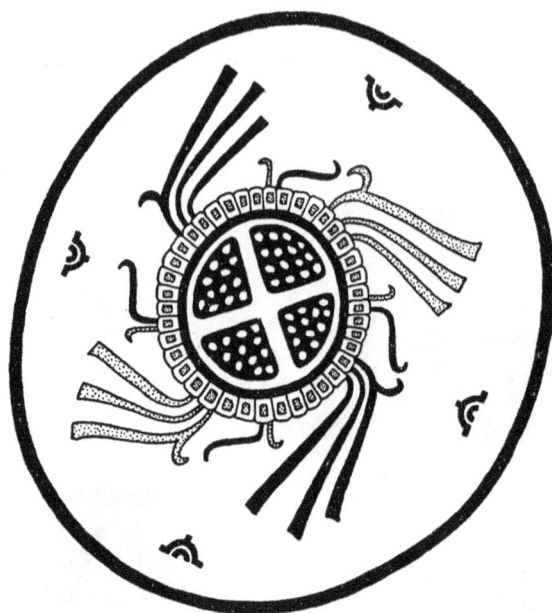

BLUE-GREEN   RED   WHITE

FIGURE 209.—Design from interior of painted gourd or wooden bowl, trench 19.

minor changes or additions which are not reflected in any other aspect of the wares. That is to say, although considerable ceramic change and intrusion of new elements is manifested in the vertical sections, there is no evidence of fundamental change of pattern or superimposition of cultures. The changes in ware frequencies and appearance of new traits can be accounted for in terms of culture growth, both of the internally stimulated and externally influenced varieties.

Tabulations of sherd counts from the two stratigraphic trenches follow. That of trench 42 is presented first (table 5). The numbers given in the columns under the various levels are the raw counts of each ware.

The first thing to be noted in the distribution chart is the clear evidence of the ceramic continuity mentioned in a preceding paragraph. Brown ware and Black ware are the most abundant forms throughout the time interval represented by the deposit (although Black ware diminishes sharply in the upper levels). Red, Red-on-Brown, and Black-and-White, the minor accompanying groups, likewise are present throughout the deposit. Had we to do with reemplacements of one culture by another, such would not be the case, obviously.   The changes must be due to other factors.

The second point of importance is the clear division of the frequencies into two major horizons, one of which can be further subdivided.   The major point of change corresponds to the 60-inch level above which there occurs Complicated Polychrome ware, along with relatively high (and apparently increasing) Polychrome tradition, accompanied by the higher frequencies of Comales, and Coarse Red-rimmed bowls.   Polychrome wares in general, and Comales and Coarse Red-rimmed bowls occur only in insignificant quantities below the 60-inch level.   This upper zone, therefore, may be taken to represent a distinct ceramic period.

Within this upper horizon no divisions can be distinguished.   The percentages of the various Polychrome wares (compared to total Polychrome of each level) are shown in table 6.

In part, perhaps, owing to small sampling, there appears to be considerable irregularity in the proportions of the several wares.   Certain trends may be noted, however, especially if we omit the 0- to 12-inch level.   Brown Polychrome appears to run along at a fairly even level; Dull Buff and Complicated Polychrome tend to decrease.   Black-on-Red Incised likewise increases at the expense of Red-on-Orange Incised, conforming to the trend of Black-and-White-on-Red.

To complete the chronologic picture, mention must be made of a member not represented by the stratitrench, i. e., the small mounds that overlie the deposit in the locality.   This was undoubtedly a continuation (with a few new traits) of the Upper horizon, since there are but few specimens in the collections which do not belong to types represented in the trenches.   This hypothetical period will be referred to as Upper II, the 0- to 60-inch horizon of the trench as Upper I.

The lower horizon can be divided into two parts, although the line of demarcation is much less sharply defined than the major division. It belongs somewhere between the 108-inch and 132-inch levels, probably nearer the latter.   The upper portion of the stratum is characterized by the presence, in small amounts, of Polychrome, Untempered ware, Comales, Coarse Red-rimmed bowls, and Polished Brown ware. As will appear from the distributions from trench 13, there are other wares distinctive of this subdivision.   This subdivision, which we may designate Lower II, corresponds roughly to the zone of low sherd occurrence.   The lower portion of the zone, Lower I, is distinguished by absence of the aforementioned wares (the lone Dull Buff Polychrome sherd in the 144- to 156-inch level is surely a stray), and the presence of relatively larger quantities of White ware.

TABLE 5.—*Depth distribution*

Wares	Upper I										Lower II			
	0–12		12–24		24–36		36–48		48–60		60–72		72–84	
	No.	Pct.	No.	Pct.	No.	Pct.	No.	Pct.	No.	Pct.	No.	Pct.	No.	Pct.
Polychrome wares:														
Dull Buff	25		96		137		152		9		1			
Complicated	10		12		37		82		9					
Brown	8		59		61		53		4					
Black-and-White-on-Red [1]	20		224		111		57		1				1	
Red-on-Orange Incised	4		19		65		123		3					
Black-on-Red Incised	2		124		96		63							
Total Polychrome [2]	81	18	546	24	527	23	496	17	28	8	1	[3]+	1	+
Untempered ware	10	2	54	2	49	2	48	1	3	+	6	2	10	2
Comales	29	6	23	1	55	2	136	4	2	+	2	+	1	+
Coarse Red-rimmed bowls	8	1	27	1	96	4	102	3	7	2	1	+		
Brown ware	183	40	925	41	948	42	1,536	53	197	57	131	64	246	63
Polished Brown ware			4	+	12	+	14	+			4	1	5	1
Red ware	96	21	565	25	364	16	340	11	8	2	9	4	30	7
Red-on-Brown	22	4	40	1	100	4	120	4	10	2	12	5	21	5
Red-on-Brown Incised ware							1	+						
Black-and-White ware	1	+			6	+	2	+	9	2	4	1	15	3
White ware									1	+			2	+
Black ware	5	1	10	+	38	1	49	1	79	22	35	16	61	15
Monumental ware	15	3	11	+	16	+	26	+	3	+			5	1
Total sherds	450		2,205		2,211		2,870		347		205		397	

[1] Including Black-on-Red ware.
[2] "Total Polychrome" includes in some cases a few painted sherds indeterminable as to ware.
[3] +, Less than 1 percent.

Trench 13 is easy to place in relation to the preceding one. Presence in small quantities of Polychrome wares, Untempered ware, Comales, and Coarse Red-rimmed bowls, fairly certainly places the section from 12 inches down as Lower II. The slightly greater quantity of Polychrome wares, and, more certainly, the presence of Complicated Polychrome, indicates that the 0- to 12-inch level represents an overlap into the Upper period. The greater amount of sherds from this trench is of value in backing up just that portion of trench 42 which is most liable to sampling error due to low sherd frequency. Three wares, one poorly represented and the other two completely absent from trench 42, appear to belong to this subhorizon: Polished Brown, which appears in greatest frequency; and Brown-and-White and Red-and-White, the minor Bichrome varieties. The absence of

TABLE 6.—*Percentages of various Polychrome wares (on basis of total Polychrome) found at each level in trench 42*

Polychrome ware	Levels (in inches)				
	0–12	12–24	24–36	36–48	48–60
Dull Buff _____percent__	30	17	24	28	32
Complicated _____do____	12	2	7	15	32
Brown _____do____	9	10	11	10	15
Black-and-White-on-Red _____do____	24	41	21	11	3
Red-on-Orange Incised _____do____	4	3	12	23	10
Black-on-Red Incised _____do____	2	22	18	11	------
Total Polychrome _____number__	81	546	527	496	28

(in inches) of wares in trench 42

Lower II—Continued								Lower I										Total number of sherds
84–96		96–108		108–120		120–132		132–144		144–156		156–168		168–180		180–192		
No.	Pct.	No.	Pct.	No.	Pct.	No.	Pct.	No.	Pct.	No.	Pct.	No.	Pct.	No.	Pct.	No.	Pct.	
		1				1												423
																		150
																		185
1																		415
7																		221
										1								285
8	2	1	+			1	+			1	+							1,691
15	4			1	+													196
1	+																	249
																		241
215	69	215	57	218	58	126	56	810	61	1,606	56	1,933	65	1,968	63	970	59	12,227
		1	+					6	+									46
8	2	6	1	12	3	8	3	45	3	103	3	96	3	90	2	49	3	1,829
10	2	17	4	15	4	9	4	57	4	122	4	46	1	39	1	26	1	666
1				3						2	+							7
4	1	15	4	12	3	6	2	20	1	30	1	24	+	73	2	19	1	240
		6	1	5	1	6	2	28	2	25	+	55	1	151	4	121	7	400
27	8	103	27	107	28	66	29	344	29	964	33	773	26	802	25	438	26	3,901
3	+							1?	+?			5	+					85
292		364		373		222		1,311		2,853		2,932		3,123		1,623		21,778

these types in Lower I of trench 42 cannot be attributed to insufficient sampling, and may therefore be assumed to be a real diagnostic feature. The distribution of wares found in trench 13 is shown in table 7.

FIGURINE STRATIGRAPHY

Despite the small amount of material, the figurines from trench 42 group quite satisfactorily. In table 8 it may be observed that the flat mold-made forms (types II and III) are restricted to the uppermost 60 inches of the cut, in other words to Upper I. Hand-made punctate subtypes A and D come from below 132 inches, i. e., Lower I. Subtypes G and H occur in Lower I and II. The remaining types represented, including the Laughing Face variants, occur in Lower II and the lower part of Upper I.

The trench 13 figurines show (table 9), as might be expected, a motley assemblage of types. The occurrence of flat mold-made types (II and III) in the uppermost foot-level confirms the deduction based on sherd-counts of a slight overlap into Upper I. Otherwise, the section conforms perfectly to its placing as Upper II, yielding punctate G and H forms and, as well, a variety of other types.

FORM FEATURES

By combining the results of the two stratigraphic trenches, the following (p. 76) vessel shapes and features can be allocated according to period:

TABLE 7.—Depth distribution (in inches) of wares in trench 13

Wares	Upper I 0–12 No.	Pct.	12–24 No.	Pct.	24–36 No.	Pct.	Lower II 36–48 No.	Pct.	48–60 No.	Pct.	60–72 No.	Pct.	72–84 No.	Pct.	84–96 No.	Pct.	96–108 No.	Pct.	108–120 No.	Pct.	120–132 No.	Pct.	Total number of sherds
Polychrome wares:																							
Dull Buff	17		10				2																29
Complicated	2																						2
Brown	8		6		4		5		3		1		4				3				3		42
Black-and-White-on-Red[1]	28		4												5								40
Red-on-Orange Incised	23		6		1		2		2				2		1						2		34
Black-on-Red Incised	12		2		2						1				1								15
Total	90	2	28	+	7	+	9	+	5	+	2	+	6	+	7	+	3	+		+	5	+	162
Untempered ware	21	1	16	1	27	1	33	1	33	1	46	1	40	1	66	1	27	1	4	1	12	1	325
Comales	8	+	3																1		3		15
Coarse Red-rimmed bowls	2	+	2	+											3		5						12
Brown ware	2,183	71	2,501	68	2,443	64	1,493	49	1,302	59	1,539	55	2,335	65	2,482	50	1,266	47	614	44	499	58	18,657
Polished Brown ware	9	+	37	1	51	1	48	1	15		13		24		24		3				1		225
Red ware	325	10	360	9	253	6	250	8	91	4	174	6	178	4	235	4	66	2	29	2	52	6	2,013
Red-on-Brown ware	10	+	92	2	100	2	123	4	101	4	127	4	236	6	278	5	86	3	36	2	23	2	1,212
Red-on-Brown Incised ware			7		9		2												1		1		21
Black ware	339	11	545	14	810	21	943	31	563	26	774	27	600	16	1,299	26	914	34	426	30	191	22	7,404
Black-and-White ware	81	2	52	1	83	2	82	2	64	2	101	3	141	3	290	4	279	10	264	18	66	7	1,493
White ware	6	+	2	+		+	6	+	3	+	1	+	12	+	4	+					3	+	39
Miscellaneous Bichrome:																							
Brown-and-White			4		4		3								4								15
Red-and-White							1				1		3										5
Total			4		4		4				1		3		4								20
Negative Painted ware			1				3						2		3								11
Monumental ware			1		2						2		2		1								6
Modern (not included in total sherds)	7																						7
Total sherds	3,073		3,651		3,791		2,996		2,168		2,780		3,579		4,696		2,649		1,375		857		31,615

[1] Including Black-on-Red ware.
[2] +, less than 1 percent.

TABLE 8.—*Depth distribution (in inches) of figurines in trench 42*

Figurines and other objects	0-12	12-24	24-36	36-48	48-60	60-72	72-84	84-96	96-108	108-120	120-132	132-144	144-156	156-168	168-180	180-192
Figurines																
I. Punctate hand-made:																
Subtype A																
Subtype D												1	2	1	1	1
Subtype G														1		
Subtype H										1					1?	1?
Subtype X		1										1	2	1	1	1
Bodies (subtypes indeterminate)	2	3	2	4	1		2					2	2	4	4	4
II. Flat mold-made (small)			2	6												
III. Flat mold-made (large)			2													
IV. Hand-made appliqué								2								
V. Mold-made appliqué																
VI. Mold-made open-backed																
VII. San Marcos mold-made																
VIII. Laughing Face B (small variants)				1		1?	1									
IX. Masks and maskettes			1?	1			1									
X. Large idols																
Miscellaneous elements																
Painted clay pellets		1	6	2												
Flute with molded ornament		1	1													

TABLE 9.—*Depth distribution (in inches) of figurines in trench 13*

Figurines	Upper I	Lower II								
	0-12	12-24	24-36	36-48	48-60	60-72	72-84	84-96	96-108	108-120
I. Punctate hand-made:										
Subtype A										
Subtype D										
Subtype G		1		2		1		4	1	1
Subtype H			1		1	1	2	1		
Subtype X		1	1		2	1		1	1	
Bodies (subtypes indeterminate)		1			1	4	2	4		1
II. Flat mold-made (small)	3									
III. Flat mold-made (large)	2									
IV. Hand-made appliqué	1	1	3	1		1?	1?	1		
V. Mold-made appliqué					1?					
VI. Mold-made open-backed	3	3		2		1?				
VII. San Marcos mold-made			1				1			
VIII. Laughing Face B (small variants)			1							
IX. Masks and maskettes										
X. Large idols	1?	2		1						

Upper I.—Tall open-spout pitchers with long vertical handles, cylindrical in cross section; long solid legs with loop foot; legs with zoomorphic ornament; relief-decorated (molded) bowl bases (Brown Polychrome).

Upper I and Lower II.—"Frying pan" incensarios; strap handles; small loop handles; tall annular bases; cylindrical cross-section hollow supports.

Lower II.—Vertical-side tripod jars with incised or relief ornament about base; bulbous-based jars with tripod supports; vessels with vertical modeled lugs; effigy vessels (?); hollow slab legs with L- or T-shaped openings; blunt conical hollow legs; low, wide hemispherical feet; small solid ball feet; supported spouts; flat horizontally placed semicircular lugs; scraped ("raspada") decoration.

Lower I and II.—Low annular bowl bases; "negative painting" (more common in II), unsupported spouts.

MINOR OBJECTS OF CLAY

Among the miscellaneous objects of baked clay, the following may be placed according to period.

Upper I.—Small painted pellets of clay; flutes with modeled ornament; mold-made spindle whorls with relief decoration.

Lower II.—Painted mold-made spindle whorls; "double rings."

On the basis of occurrence in the small mounds in the vicinity of trench 42, the clay "pipe lines" can probably be assigned safely to **Upper II.**

ANALYSIS OF MOUND MATERIALS

The material from the mound mass of the several mounds trenched has been subjected to gross analysis, that is, a determination of wares represented. In view of the fact that the mounds are themselves secondary deposits, it was not considered worth while to save all the sherds for counts, etc. Only decorated sherds, rims, bases, and restorable vessels were saved. All figurines, however fragmentary, and miscellaneous objects of clay were saved as well. On the basis of this material, it is possible to place the various cuts in relation to the established ceramic column or, at least, to give them minimal period datings.

Inspection of the ware occurrences shown in table 10 indicates that most of the mounds of the Central Group belong to Lower II, containing as they do small amounts of Polychrome and related wares, little White ware, and the varied figurine types characteristic of this period. In several instances there was a thin superficial layer of later (Upper I) material, as Stirling was able to observe in the field. This material was not segregated, however, nor was it possible to determine whether it represented a final enlargement of the mound, or was occupational debris resulting from a mound-dwelling habit such as prevails at the present day in the region. Most or all of these mounds had been plowed and cultivated within recent years, making inspection of their superficial layers impossible.

The mound cuts in the northwest sector of the site, the Small Mound Group, yielded quantities of late material. Owing to heavy field culling, we do not have a complete sample of wares represented, but the large amounts of Polychrome sherds indicate an Upper period dating, and the occurrence of several types not represented in the stratitrenches, Fine-line Black-on-White and varieties of Tan Polychrome, point to an even later position than the upper layers of the stratigraphic sections. As a matter of fact, the period Upper II is based chiefly on the material from these mounds.

CACHE ASSOCIATIONS

The largest quantity of cache material comes from the burials and offerings of trenches 30 and 34. The material from trench 30 is described in table 12.

It is clear from the absence of Polychrome and associated wares that all the trench 30 burial material belongs to the Lower horizon. The presence of "scraped" decoration on Black ware vessels (II-7), Polished Brown ware (II-19), supported spouts (II-5, II-19), and absence of White ware, taken all together, point fairly surely to Lower II for the placing of the material. The temporal difference between the two parts of the mound—the base and the superstructure—

TABLE 10.—*Ware occurrence in Mound Groups*

Wares	Occurrence[1] in indicated trench in—										
	Central Mound Group								Small Mound Group		
	12	15	30	31	32	32 B	33	34	14	19	41
Polychrome wares:											
Dull Buff	S	S	S	S	S	----	+	S	+	+	+
Brown	S	S	S	S	S	----	+	S	+	+	+
Black-and-White-on-Red	----	----	S	----	----	----	S	----	+	+	+
Black-on-Red	S	----	----	----	S	----	S	S	+	+	+
Complicated	----	----	----	----	----	----	S	----	+	+	+
Red-on-Orange Incised	----	S	----	----	S	----	----	----	+	+	+
Black-on-Red Incised	----	S	----	----	S	----	S	----	+	+	+
Untempered ware	+	+	+	+	+	+	+	+	+	+	+
Comales	----	----	+	----	+	----	+	----	+	+	+
Coarse Red-rimmed bowls	----	----	----	----	----	----	+	----	+	+	+
Brown ware	+	+	+	+	+	+	+	+	+	+	+
Polished Brown ware	----	----	+	S	----	S	S	+	----	----	----
Red ware	+	+	+	+	+	+	+	+	----	+	+
Red-on-Brown Incised ware	----	+	+	+	+	+	+	+	----	+	----
Black-and-White ware	+	+	+	+	+	+	+	+	----	----	+
White ware	----	S	+	S	S	----	S	+	----	----	----
Black ware	+	+	+	+	+	+	+	+	+	----	+
Monumental ware	+	+	+	+	+	S	+	+	----	+	+
Stucco Painted ware	----	----	+	----	----	----	----	----	----	----	----
Negative Painted ware	----	----	S	S	----	S	----	----	----	----	----

[1] +, Present; S, present in small quantity only.

TABLE 11.—*Occurrence of figurines and other objects in Mound Groups*

Figurines and other objects	Occurrence[1] in indicated trench in—										
	Central Mound Group							Small Mound Group			
	12	15	30	31	32	33	34	14	14-A	19	41
Figurines											
I. Punctate hand-made:	+	+	+	+	----	+	+	----	----	----	----
Subtype A	----	+	+	+	----	+	+	----	----	----	----
Subtype D	----	----	+	+	----	+	+	----	----	----	----
Subtype G	----	----	+	+	----	+	+	----	----	----	----
Subtype H	+	----	+	+	----	+	----	----	----	----	----
Subtype X	+	----	+	+	----	+	----	----	----	----	----
Bodies (subtype indeterminate)	+	----	+	+	----	+	----	----	----	----	----
II. Flat mold-made (small)	----	+	----	----	----	+	+	+	----	+	+
III. Flat mold-made (large)	----	----	----	----	----	+	+	----	----	+	+
IV. Hand-made appliqué	----	----	----		----	----	+	----	----	----	----
V. Mold-made appliqué	----	----	----	----	----	----	----	----	----	----	----
VI. Mold-made open-backed	----	----	----	----	----	----	----	----	----	----	----
VII. San Marcos mold-made	----	----	----	----	----	----	+	----	----	----	----
VIII. Laughing Face B (small variants)	+	----	----	+?	----	----	+	----	----	----	----
IX. Masks and maskettes	----	----	----	----	----	----	----	----	----	----	----
X. Large idols	+	+	----	+	----	----	+	----	----	+	----
Miscellaneous elements											
Painted clay pellets	----	----	----	----	----	[1]+	----	----	----	+	+
Spindle whorls with molded ornament	----	----	+	----	----	+	+	----	----	+	+
Flutes with molded ornament	----	----	----	----	----	----	+	----	----	----	----
Zoomorphic vessel supports	----	----	----	----	----	----	+?	----	----	+	+
Thin solid slab legs, sometimes stepped	----	+	+	----	----	----	----	----	----	+	+
Hollow slab legs	+	+	+	----	----	----	+	----	----	+	+
Relief-decorated bowl base	----	+	+	----	----	----	----	+	----	----	----

[1] +, Present.
[2] With shallow, apparently intrusive burial.

TABLE 12.—*Cache material from burials of trench 30*

Burial No.	Ceramic associations			
	No.	Ware	Shape	Decoration
II-5	1	Brown	Open convex-side bowl (miniature)	Post-firing incised.
	1	Black	Incurved-side bowl (miniature)	Do.
	2	do	Squat body, long neck, vertical supported spout.	None.
	3	Black-and-White (white rim).	Open convex-side bowls	Do.
II-7	1	Black	Wide vertical-side jar	Scraped ("raspada").
II-9	1	do	Slender jar (miniature)	Post-firing incised.
II-10	1	Black-and-White (white rim).	Open convex-side bowl (miniature)	None.
II-12-(Face only)	1	Red	Slightly flaring side jar (not restorable).	Do.
	1	Black (cover)		Do.
II-13	2	Brown	1 wide-mouth jar, 1 shallow flaring-side bowl.	Do.
II-14 (Face only)	1	Red-on-Brown	Jar (?)	Do.
II-16	1	Brown	Wide-mouth jar	Do.
II-17 (Face only)	1	Plain ware	Vertical-side jar	Do.
	1	Black-and-White (white rim).	Open convex-side bowl	Do.
II-18	3	Black	Concave side, annular-base jars	Post-firing incised.
	2	Brown	Vertical-side, bulbous-base jars	None.
	2	Red-on-Brown	Vertical-side, bulbous-base jars	Do.
	4	Stuccoed	(2) Vertical-side, bulbous-base jars	Small element designs in green, black outline, on red ground.
				(1) One end red, center and opposite end green.
			(2) Potstands	(1) Ends red; center striped red, green, yellow, black.
II-19	2	Polished Brown	Low base with tall, slender necks (reworked supported-spout vessels).	(1) Pre-firing incised.
II-20	1	Black-and-White	Open convex-side bowl	(Rude) pre-firing incised.

cannot have been great, for material from both falls into the same subperiod. The fortunate circumstance of being able to place the Stucco ware chronologically will aid us in relating the Cerro de las Mesas ceramic column to those of adjacent regions.

The bulk of the ceramic material from trench 34 consisted of the pots containing assortments of marine shells, etc. Some of these were of the poorly fired Plain ware jars, unplaced in our ware chronology; others were slightly concave-walled flat-based tripod jars, of Brown ware and Polished Brown ware, indicating an allocation of Lower II. The spectacular jade cache, the quantities of Monumental ware (idols and pedestals), and the painted material, therefore, are assignable to this period. It must be pointed out, however, that the Monumental ware does not belong to Lower II alone, but can be shown to have continued through to Upper II.

It is possible that the superficial layers of the mound, which, as will be recalled, was repeatedly enlarged, belong to Upper I, for a fair amount of Polychrome wares and Upper I figurines came from the surface few inches. On the other hand, this material may be unconformable surface material, mixed in by plowing. Modern residence habits favor the aboriginal mounds as bases for dwellings, and this custom may have prevailed anciently as well.

NONCERAMIC ELEMENTS

While the present report is primarily concerned with pottery and pottery sequences, there are a few nonceramic traits on whose occurrence we have sufficient data to relate them chronologically.

The spectacular and important jade cache from trench 34 has been placed in Lower II on the basis of the ceramic content of the mound. Smaller quantities of jade were encountered, associated with certain burials in trench 30 (see burial inventories, p. 9), assigned to the same period. Occasional pieces only were found in other trenches, none in the cuts in the Upper period Small Mound locality. Apparently, in Lower II jade was more abundant than at any other time. The variation in color and quality of the jade—from clear almost grass-green to dull-gray shades—suggests that it may come from a number of different sources, indicating extensive trade relations in this period.

Use of stucco is another trait that has temporal significance, although according to quantity rather than mere presence. In Lower II mounds, occasional floors, etc., are faced with this material, but most of the floors, stairways, and other features were faced with clay. It is in the latest structures, those of Upper II, that this material is most abundant. As to types of structures, little can be said, for few could be worked out in detail. The most distinctive architectural type on which we have information is that of rather long narrow floor plan, with bays or niches in the walls, known from trenches 32, 34, and 14, in short, from Lower II to Upper II times.

The occurrence of stone yokes and hachas in deposits of known relation to the ceramic column is of no slight importance for coast archeology. The yoke (trench 30), it is true, is plain, as is another in the purchase collection; the hacha (from trench 34) is elaborately carved. Both belong to Lower II cache lots—the same period in which occur the small variants of Laughing Face figurines, and presumably those of the classic variety which come from nearby Cerro del Gallo. If these several types of objects actually form a complex, or part of a complex, as has been suggested in the past, we have for the first time a definite temporal placing for it.

UNPLACED ELEMENTS

There are a few objects in the collections from purchase sources which are not represented in the excavations. Among these are two bottles, one of Plain ware, one of Black ware, with vertical handles and appliqué Tlaloc faces, of the type found on the slopes of the volcanoes of the Highland (pl. 24). Presumably they are referable to Upper I. The Aztec-type figurines have already been mentioned. They probably relate to Upper II. The one Plumbate vessel recovered, because of its intrusive location, cannot be placed, nor can it serve for dating purposes—it may very well have been preserved for a considerable time before its placing in the pit.

COMPARATIVE ANALYSIS AND CHRONOLOGY

This final chapter aims at an interpretation of the data presented on this site in the Mistequilla of Veracruz. In accordance with the goal originally stated, this interpretation will attempt to place the site on the basis of its ceramics both in relation to neighboring and better-known cultures and in time. To do this, we shall pass in review the Cerro de las Mesas horizons established on the basis of stratigraphy, together with their principal diagnostic features.

Stratigraphic excavations in refuse deposits have served to establish two main ceramic periods which we have designated Upper and Lower. The Lower divides into two subperiods, I and II, and a subdivision of the Upper has been marked off on the basis of the slightly divergent content of mounds which overlie deposits containing Upper I material. It must be made clear that the differentiation into periods and subperiods has no connotation of populational change or succession of cultures. If the ceramic evidence can be taken as representative of the total culture, we have to do with a single culture and presumably population, in which patterns changed owing to normal processes of internal culture growth and absorption of external influences.

The characteristics of the various temporal divisions can be listed briefly. For purposes of presentation, we shall begin with the earliest, Lower I. The ceramic pattern is an essentially simple one, consisting mainly of Monochrome wares: Brown, Red, Black, and White, with one Bichrome, Red-on-Brown. Small amounts of Negative Painted ware, usually Red-on-Brown, more rarely Black-on-White, are found in this horizon also. The most common vessel shapes are simple silhouette shallow bowls; composite silhouette bowls also occur, but less commonly. Tripod supports (hollow subconical legs) and occasional "ring" (low annular) bases, and spouted vessels occur, as well. Decoration, aside from the simple angular patterns of Red-on-Brown ware and the lines and dots of Negative Painted ware, consists in geometric incising. Red paint was often rubbed into the grooves to accentuate the pattern. Figurines, to judge by the limited sampling at our disposal, consisted of the hand-made type with punctations to represent features, common all along the east coast from the Huasteca to the Maya area. Specifically, the forms represented are variants of that designated Tres Zapotes subtype A, an unspecialized form, which is of long duration at that site, first appearing in the Lower period; of another designated Tres Zapotes subtype D, which belongs to the Middle and possibly Upper periods at the type station; and two specialized local forms (G and H), which fit typologically into the elaborated varieties of Middle Tres Zapotes.

In the following period, Lower II, the same wares (except for White ware, which nearly disappears) and types continue, with the addition of certain new elements. A painted ware, called "Untempered" because of its distinctive paste type, which is related on the one hand to Tres Zapotes Polychrome and on the other to late wares of central and northern Veracruz and to Fine Orange, appears in small quantities, along with certain local Polychromes, a "Stucco Painted" ware, and miscellaneous varieties of Bichrome. None of these innovations is abundant. In regard to vessel forms, there appear concave-side jars, with ornaments about the base, and frequently with hollow slab legs—a shape-type strongly reminiscent of Teotihuacán. Slender jars with bulbous bases and tripod supports also appear on this level. In addition to the normal type of incising, there occurs a broad-line "scraped" decoration. Figurine types are quite varied. In addition to local specializations of the hand-made punctate pattern, there appear forms referable to Rancho de las Animas, and, as well, a variety of mold-made types, including elaborate variant Laughing Face forms. While there is undoubtedly a chronological succession of these forms, we are unfortunately not able to define it on the basis of the material at hand. Obviously, Cerro de las Mesas received influences from various quarters, and what with the effects of time lag in diffusion, and perhaps the conservatism of a peripheral site, some traits co-occur there which in their original sources are probably sharply differentiated in time. In addition to figurines, there appear for the first time large free-modeled idols of clay, which have been included with their elaborate pedestals under the head of "Monumental ware." Belonging to this period are the only examples of stone yokes and hachas recovered.

As in the preceding instance, the change from Lower II to Upper I is marked not by change of wares and types but rather by the addition of new elements, accompanied by changes in emphasis, i. e., quantitative changes, on certain wares. Polychrome wares in general become more numerous, and there appears a new variety, Complicated Polychrome, which is very closely related to the Cholula ware designated by Noguera as "Cerámica polícroma laca." Zoomorphic vessel legs,

bowls with molded decoration on the base, and very flat molded figurines unmistakably of Cholulteca type accompany this Highland
ware, apparently integral parts of the transported complex.   Black-
and-White-on-Red ware is a pretty certain indicator of Highland influence.   There is also a Black-on-Red Incised ware, common, to judge
by the number of examples figured, in Cerro Montoso deposits, as well
as in Cholulteca and late Valley of Mexico sites.   Flutes with modeled
ornaments (painted pellets of clay) are among the diagnostic features
of the period.

Upper II is, as has been stated, an imperfectly defined unit, based
chiefly on material from mounds superimposed on Upper I strata.
Of nonceramic features, greatest use of stucco for structural purposes
and presence of copper (small quantities only have been found) are
outstanding.   As far as we can tell, there is but little ceramic change;
handles with zoomorphic ornament, tall pitchers with vertically placed
cylindrical handles, stepped flat slab legs, large clay tubes, and a few
pieces of Tan Polychrome ware (a type represented on the Isla de
los Sacrificios) are the only new features.   Probably the few Aztec
figurines collected from the surface of the site, surely trade pieces,
are referable to this period.

In the absence of internal evidence from the deposits themselves,
we are forced to rely on comparative evidence for the chronological
placing of the Cerro de las Mesas ceramic column.   Fortunately,
there are a series of traits which are not just resemblances but are
identical to diagnostic features of established sequences elsewhere.
It can be shown that the order of appearance of these imported traits
at Cerro de las Mesas conforms quite well to their sequence in their
presumed centers of origin, a fact which justified their use as time
markers.

Beginning again with the earliest local period, we find two Highland
elements, Negative Painting and Incised Outline Red-on-Brown ware.[9]
The former occurs in Teotihuacán I, the latter, a more specific parallel,
in Teotihuacán late II—early III.   The figurine types, or rather subtypes, are all of them referable to Middle Tres Zapotes.   These elements in combination, suggest a beginning date corresponding approximately with that of Teotihuacán III for the earliest defined period at
Cerro de las Mesas.

Lower II similarly has some features of probably Highland pro-
venience.   Most, if not all, of these belong to Teotihuacán late III to
IV–V: concave-walled jars with hollow slab legs, and ornaments about
basal angle; vessels with vertical modeled lugs (also Upper Tres
Zapotes); supported-spout vessels (also Upper Tres Zapotes); stucco-
painted ware; elaborate mold-made figurines (technique rather than

---

[9] The writer is indebted to Dr. Noguera for information as to the temporal placing of
these and other Teotihuacán elements referred to here.

detail of type is critical here). In addition to these features, we find figurines of a type related to those of Rancho de las Animas, for which a late Teotihuacán dating has been suggested, and variants of the well-known Laughing Face figurine pattern, which recur in Upper Tres Zapotes.[10] It seems reasonable enough, all in all, to propose for Lower II a rough contemporaneity with the final epochs of Teotihuacán, especially since it is followed directly, in Upper I, by Cholulteca elements. More puzzling in their suggested temporal relationships are a number of Monte Albán II elements: potstands, "raspada" decoration, and certain specific vessel shapes—tall slender spouted forms, squat tripod jars ("stucco" paint is also referable to this period at Monte Albán). Undoubtedly, these traits represent survivals in a peripheral region.

The identification of the Complicated Polychrome ware of Upper I as a direct derivative of the Cholulteca I (and II) lacquer ware need not be gone into at length here.[11] Its companion elements—zoomorphic vessel supports, relief-decorated (molded) bowl bases, flutes with modeled ornament, the low-relief molded figurines (which include Tlalocs, typical of Cholulteca I–II)—establish the source of influence beyond question of doubt (Noguera, 1937). Presence of Black-on-Red Incised ware, which is known also from late Valley of Mexico sites and Cerro Montoso (a few examples have been found associated with the late Soncautla complex at Tres Zapotes), corroborates the temporal equation of Upper I with Cholulteca I.[12] The only anomalous feature is the absence (in any Cerro de las Mesas horizon) of the ware with "decoración negra sobre fondo color natural del barro," common in Cholulteca I. Perhaps this was an everyday ware not deemed worth carrying long distances for trade, or worth imitating. The Dull Buff Polychrome resembles it closely in characteristic application of paint directly on an unprepared vessel surface, and probably replaces the Highland ware in the local pattern.

Upper II, with its Isla de los Sacrificios linkages, pitchers with cylindrical vertical handles (Mixtec, late Valley of Mexico), stepped slab vessel supports (Cholulteca II, Aztec), and copper (Cerro Montoso, etc.) is unquestionably late. Its terminal date may be assumed, however, to fall short of Conquest times by a brief space, chiefly on the basis of the scarcity of the copper objects so abundant in Veracruz at the time of the arrival of the Spaniards.[13] Probably it would be safe to place this final phase as the equivalent of most of Cholulteca II, and of all but the last of the Aztec periods of the Valley of Mexico.

---

[10] San Marcos type figurines, characteristic of Upper Tres Zapotes, also occur in this level.

[11] Examples of this ware occur in Joyce, 1927, pp. 119, 121.

[12] Specimens in Museo Nacional de México; Strebel, 1885–1889, passim.

[13] Nothing suggesting contact or early colonial material was found by us, or seen in the region.

In effect, there exists at Cerro de las Mesas a continuous ceramic column extending back from the fifteenth century to a point roughly equivalent to that of the beginning of Teotihuacán III. It is unfortunate that Teotihuacán culture, a dynamic civilization from which surged waves of influences far and wide over Mexico, has been so difficult to date on empiric evidence. So far, we have only speculative estimates for its placing. If the Cerro de las Mesas stelae with 9th Cycle dates were clearly associated with any single phase at the site, we would have a clean-cut dating not only for Cerro de las Mesas but for whichever Highland period that phase was affiliated with. In view of the occurrence of these monuments along with others of distinct art styles, and all on a many-times rebuilt plaza, they cannot be assigned with assurance to any one period. It is tempting to consider the implications of a Lower I placing of the stones. Lower I, and consequently Teotihuacán late II–early III, would perforce be carried back to the sixth century (according to the Thompson correlation). Such a placing would fit the Lower I–Middle Tres Zapotes contemporaneity established on figurine correspondences, for Middle Tres Zapotes has been dated 400–800 A. D. on the basis of linkages to the well-dated Petén. However, in the Veracruz area, where stone monuments were dragged about and reused long after their origin, it is difficult, if not impossible, to relate them to any particular ceramic horizon.

In one sense, the Cerro de las Mesas explorations contribute but little to our knowledge of Veracruz archeology. It is scarcely to be expected that the diagnostic features of its ceramics will be found to be widespread in the State.[14] Rather we have to do with an enclave of Highland culture, transplanted to the coast. Emphasis has been put, in the foregoing discussion, on relationships of the Upper period wares and figurines to those of late Cholula, but undoubtedly one should read "late Mixteca" for "Cholulteca." It is only because the Puebla site is so well known that ceramic parallels to it stand out with such prominence. The strong ties of Cholula to Tlaxcala and southward to the heart of the Mixteca in Oaxaca (cf. Noguera, 1937) make such an interpretation valid. In short, the modern designation of the Cerro de las Mesas region as the "Mistequilla" undoubtedly has a sound ethnic derivation.

Just when this Highland immigration occurred is difficult to state. Certainly there was a strong influx at the end of Lower II, which resulted in the modified ceramic patterns of Upper I. It will be recalled that features reminiscent of Teotihuacán IV (which underlies the Cholulteca material at Cholula) and certain Monte Albán-

---

[14] However, Sr. Payón, of the Instituto de Antropología e Historia, has informed me that his excavations at Cempoala reveal a great number of linkages to the Cerro de las Mesas Upper, and to the late periods of Cholula.

like traits, however, characterize the phase designated Lower II. Since this phase is not sharply set off from its predecessor, but rather emerges gradually from it, we must look to the earliest levels of Cerro de las Mesas for a previous set of Highland influences, and possibly immigrations, which were renewed at the end of Lower II and which continued to the end of the prehistoric occupation of the site.

There are, nonetheless, certain findings which do bear upon the prehistory of the Veracruz coast. We may begin by considering the quantity and type of relationships between this site and Tres Zapotes, less than 100 miles away in an air line. Aside from the elements imported to both from outside sources, we find these to be, for the most part, simple generic features, demonstrably early at Tres Zapotes, and where data are available, widespread in the region. To this category belong such features as the prevalence of Brown and Black wares, simple and composite silhouette vessels, Black-and-White ware, and the hand-made punctate-featured figurine pattern. Aside from these early presumably basic elements of regional culture, there are very few indications of direct contact between the two sites. The sloughs and swamps of intervening drainage systems patently have barred contact. Very likely, the same situation prevails northward along the coast, and for the same reason; Strebel's results, numerous localized patterns apparently coexistent in central Veracruz with one or the other of the two major cultures of Cerro Montoso and Rancho de las Animas, seem to bear out this hypothesis. In short, Highland cultures were for the coast-dwellers more accessible, for practical purposes nearer, than those of people on the other side of a river valley. Whether the same is true of the region of the long terrace systems flanking the escarpment of the mountains is as yet unknown, and in default of detailed local knowledge, unpredictable. Perhaps this zone formed a north-south highway for culture transfer, feeding the side roads, to continue the figure, which branched off to each interriverine region of the coast.

Of more than slight importance, from the areal point of view, is the occurrence of stone yokes, hachas, and Laughing Face figurines in Lower II. If these objects actually constitute a complex, as has been surmised from their nearly coterminous distribution, that complex obviously cannot be identified with the historic Totonac. Totonac archeology is more likely Cerro Montoso, as Spinden (1933) has suggested, and/or a series of the affiliated local specializations that Strebel has described.

The history of the so-called Untempered ware, with its suggested relationship to Tres Zapotes Polychrome, late central and northern Veracruz ceramics, and Fine Orange deserves not only attention but serious investigation. This ware, with its distinctive paste type (and therefore presumably distinct technology of preparation and firing), its separate set of shapes, and different slip and paint types hints at a center of development as yet unknown. Central and northern Veracruz, as well as the southern part of the State, cry out for archeological investigation. Strebel's work, admirable for its day, does not satisfy modern standards of research.

To summarize, the excavations at Cerro de las Mesas suggest solutions of various regional problems—the extent of certainty varies in each case. The following chart presents these results in graphic form. It aims at coordinating data in the light of present knowledge, and, like sailing schedules, is "subject to revision without notice" as additional information from the area may demand. The column of Mexico-Puebla sequences has been taken from published sources; that referring to Central Veracruz is, of course, a hypothetical reconstruction. In the chart, solid horizontal lines indicate major culture changes; broken lines, transitions from one to another horizon of the same culture.

| | Mexico–Puebla | Southern Veracruz | | Central Veracruz |
		Cerro de las Mesas	Tres Zapotes	
1500	Cholulteca III. Aztec III–IV.	(Unoccupied).	(Unoccupied).	Isla de los Sacrificios, Cempoala (Historic Totonac).
		Upper II.		
	Cholulteca II. Aztec I–II.	Upper I.	Soncautla complex.	Cerro Montoso (Totonac) and minor local patterns.
	Cholulteca I. Mazapan, etc.		(Unoccupied).	
1000	Teotihuacán IV–V.	Lower II.	Upper Tres Zapotes.	Yoke-hacha-Laughing Face complex.
500	Teotihuacán III.	Lower I.	Middle Tres Zapotes.	Rancho de las Animas.
	Teotihuacán II.	(Unoccupied).	Lower Tres Zapotes.	Beginnings of local specialization, stemming from Basic Coastal Pattern?
1 A.D.	Teotihuacán I.			
	Early Middle Cultures.			
	Preceramic Highland Pattern?	Basic Coastal Pattern extending from (at least) Playa de los Muertos to the Petén to southern Veracruz, and, perhaps, on to Central Veracruz.		

FIGURE 210.—Chart of culture sequences at Cerro de las Mesas, based on ceramic data.

BIBLIOGRAPHY

CASO, A.
    1938. Exploraciones en Oaxaca, temporado 1936–37. Inst. Panam. Geog. é Hist., Publ. No. 34. Mexico.
DRUCKER, PHILIP
    1943. Ceramic sequences from Tres Zapotes, Veracruz, Mexico. Bur. Amer. Ethnol. Bull. 140.
GALDO, Y VILLA, J.
    1912. Las Ruinas de Cempoala . . . An. Mus. Nac., vol. 3, App. pp. xcv–clxii.
JOYCE, THOMAS A.
    1927. Maya and Mexican art. London.

LINNÉ, S.
    1934. Archaeological researches at Teotihuacán, Mexico. Stockholm.
NOGUERA, E.
    1935. La cerámica de Tenayuca y las excavaciones estratigráphicas. *In*
        Tenayuca, Estudio Arqueólogico, Dept. de Mon. de la Sec. de Ed.
        Publ., pp. 140–201.
    1937. Conclusiones principales obtenidas por el estudio de la cerámica arque-
        ólogica de Cholula, Mexico. (Mimeographed.)
    1937 a. El Altar de los Craneos Esculpidos de Cholula, Mexico.
NOVELO, R. J. CABALLOS
    1928. Cempoala. *In* Estado Actual de los . . . Edificios . . . , Sec. de Ed.
        Publ., pp. 43–61.
NUTTALL, ZELIA
    1910. The Island of Sacrificios. Amer. Anthrop., n. s., vol. 12, pp, 257–295.
SAVILLE, M. H.
    1916. The glazed ware of Central America. *In* Holmes Anniv. Vol., pp.
        421–426.
SELER, EDWARD
    1915. Die Teotiuacan-Kultur des Hochlands von Mexiko. Gesamm. Abhandl.,
        bd. 5, pp. 405–585. Berlin.
SPINDEN, E. S.
    1933. The place of Tajín in Totonac archaeology. Amer. Anthrop., n. s., vol.
        35, pp. 225–270.
SPINDEN, HERBERT J.
    1927. Study dead city of "Rubber People." N. Y. Times, Sunday, May 1.
STIRLING, MATTHEW W.
    1940. Great stone faces of the Mexican jungle. Nat. Geogr. Mag., vol. 78,
        No. 3, pp. 309–334.
    1941. Expedition unearths buried masterpieces of carved jade. Nat. Geogr.
        Mag., vol. 80, No. 3, pp. 277–302.
    1943. Stone monuments of Southern Mexico. Bur. Amer. Ethnol. Bull. 138.
STREBEL, H.
    1884. Die Ruinen von Cempoallen . . . Abhandl. des Naturwiss. Vereins. zu
        Hamburg, vol. 8, pt. 1.
    1885–1889. Alt-Mexiko. Archäol Beitr. z. Kulturgesch. Seiner Bewohner. 2
        vols. Hamburg u. Leipzig.
VAILLANT, GEORGE C.
    1935. Chronology and stratigraphy in the Maya area. Maya Res., vol. 2,
        pp. 119–143.
    1938. A correlation of archaeological and historical sequences in the Valley
        of Mexico. Amer. Anthrop., n. s., vol. 40, No. 4, pp. 535–573.
    1941. The Aztecs of Mexico. N. Y.
WEIANT, C. W.
    1943. An introduction to the ceramics of Tres Zapotes, Veracruz, Mexico.
        Bur. Amer. Ethnol. Bull. 139.

INDEX

○

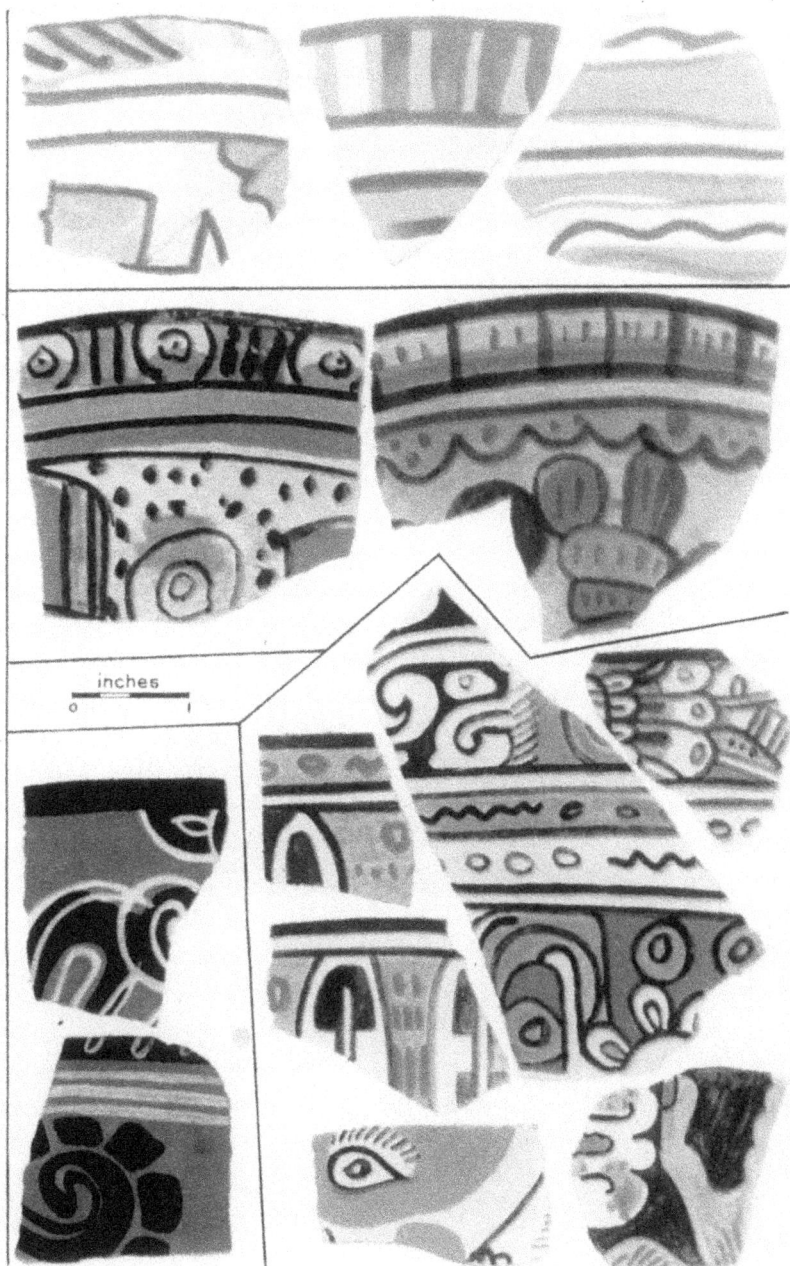

CERRO DE LAS MESAS POLYCHROME WARES.   DULL BUFF POLYCHROME, BROWN
POLYCHROME, BLACK-AND-WHITE-ON-RED, AND COMPLICATED POLYCHROME.

COMPLICATED POLYCHROME SHERDS: JAR EXTERIORS. BOWL INTERIOR.

BROWN POLYCHROME BOWL SHERDS.

TRADE WARES.

a, b, White-on-Cream ware; *c-f*, Fine-line Black-on-White.   (Photographed from water-color paintings of sherds.)

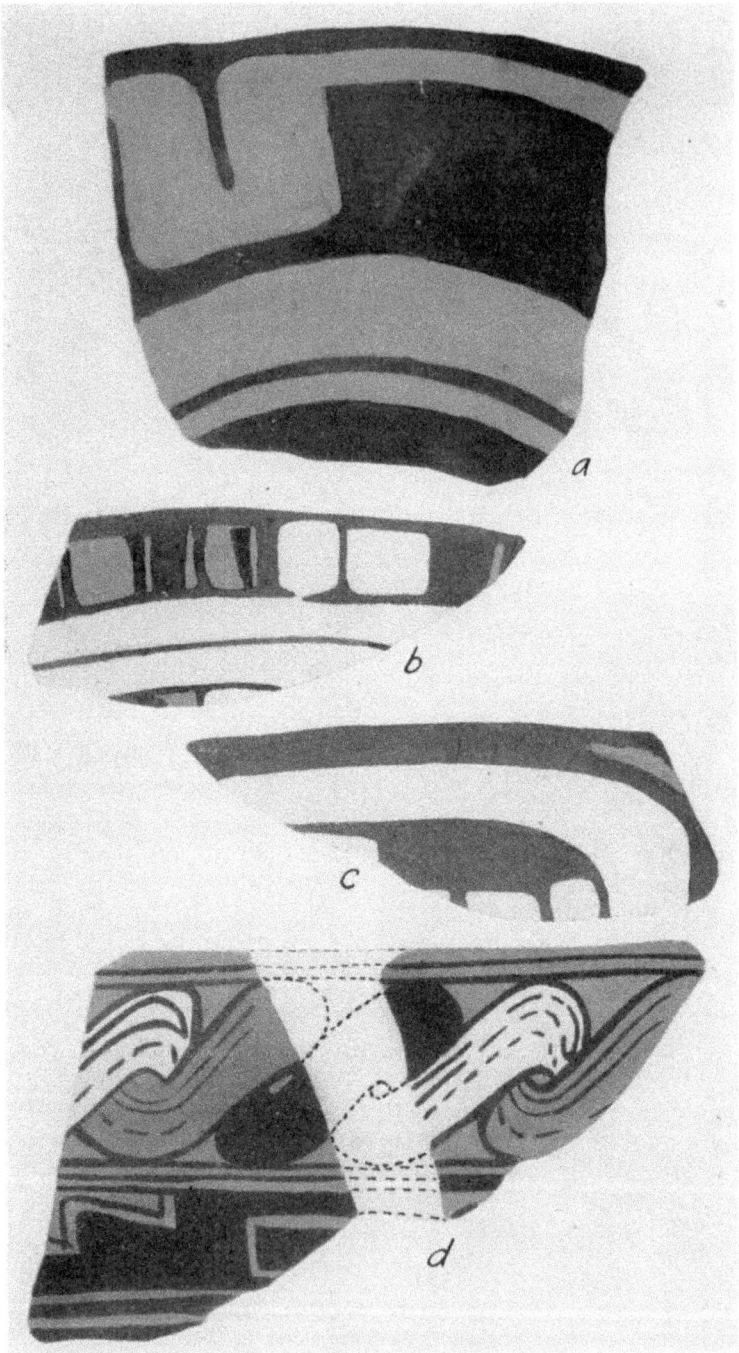

TRADE WARES.

a, b, c, Cerro Montoso (Totonac): *a,* Brown (misfired Black?)-on-Cinnamon-Buff; *b, c,*
Black-White-and-Orange-on-Buff.   *d,* Mixteca Polychrome; Red-White-Black-and-
Gray-on-Orange. (Photographed from water-color paintings.)

TRENCH 30. OBJECTS ASSOCIATED WITH BURIAL 11-18.

a, Pottery vessels; *b*, yoke and figurines to north of vessels. Arrow in *a* shows location (in the bank) of yoke and figurines.

a, Stucco floor, trench 31.

b, Buried stairway, trench 33.

TRENCHES 31 AND 33

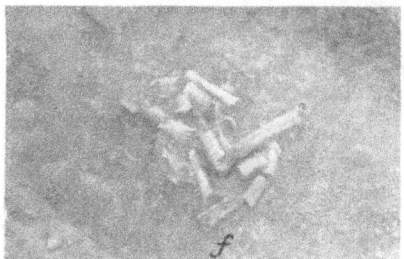

MONUMENTAL WARE FROM TRENCHES 7 AND 34.

a, *b*, *d*, Trench 7.   *c*, *e*, *f*, Trench 34, showing different views of single lot of fragments
c, pedestal and various fragments; *e*, head found inside pedestal; *f*, covering of fragments
of arms and legs.

VIEWS OF JADE CACHE, TRENCH 34

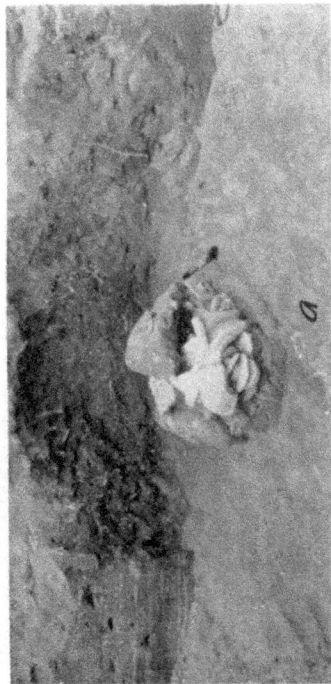

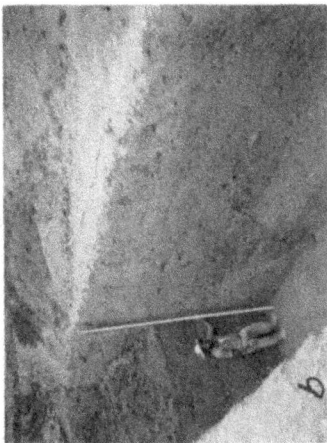

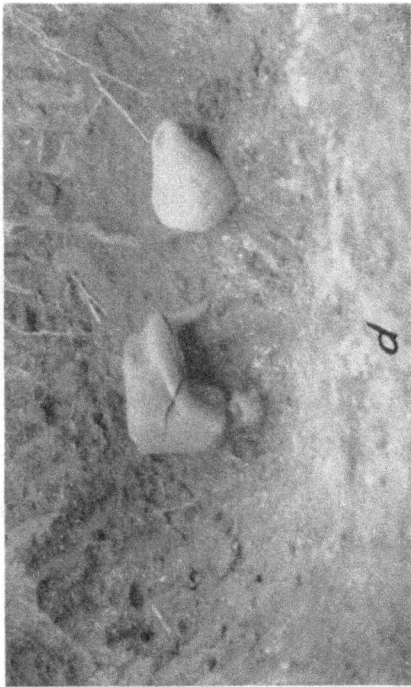

TRENCHES 34, 13, 14–A, AND 15

a, View of jade cache, trench 34; b, trench 13; c, remnants of pipe-line, trench 14–A; d, Plumbate vessel in intrusive pit, trench 15.

TRENCH 40.

a and *b*, Ollas containing skulls; *b* shows relation to stucco layers.

Trench 42.

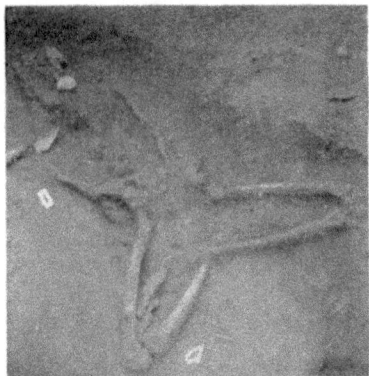

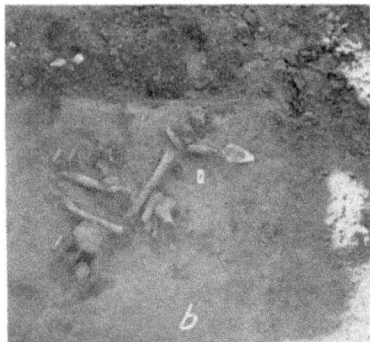

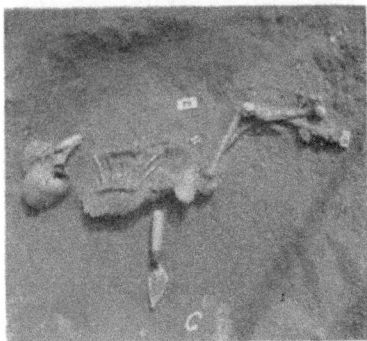

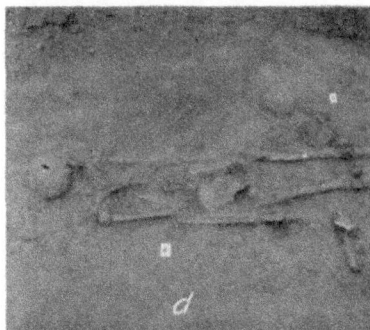

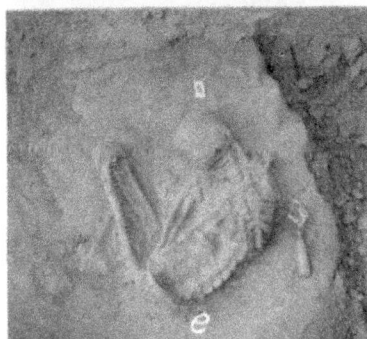

BURIALS I–1 TO I–6 (*a–f*).

BULLETIN 141 PLATE 14

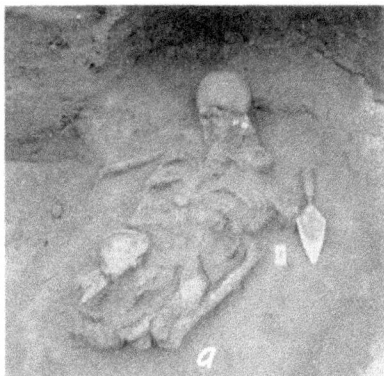

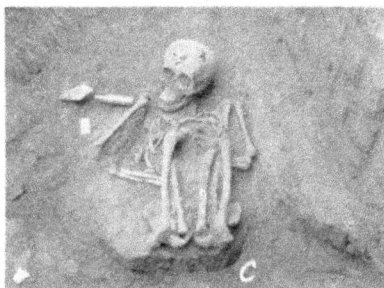

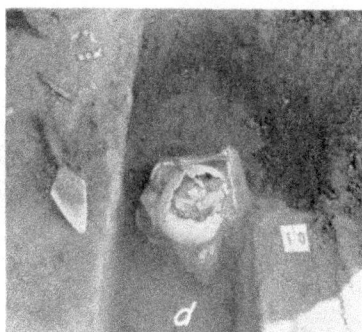

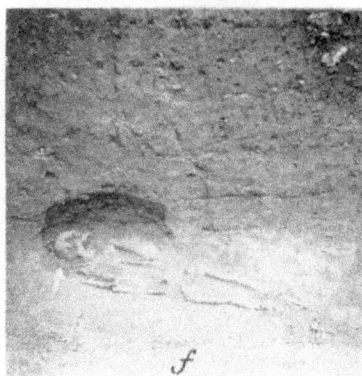

BURIALS I-7 TO I-10 (*a–d*); BURIAL I-14 (*e*); BURIAL I-16 (*f*).

BROWN WARE VESSELS.

a, From trench 34; *b*, *d*, *e*, *f*, from burial II–3; *c*, from burial I–5; *g*, from trench 30; *h*, from burial II–20. (Scale of *h* slightly smaller than remainder.)

BROWN WARE VESSELS.

a, From trench 34; *b*, from trench 34 (contained collection of shells etc.); *c*, *d*, from burial I–18; *e*, a unique form; *f*, from trench 34 (contained collection of shells etc.); *g*, from trench 13, at 60 to 72-inch level.

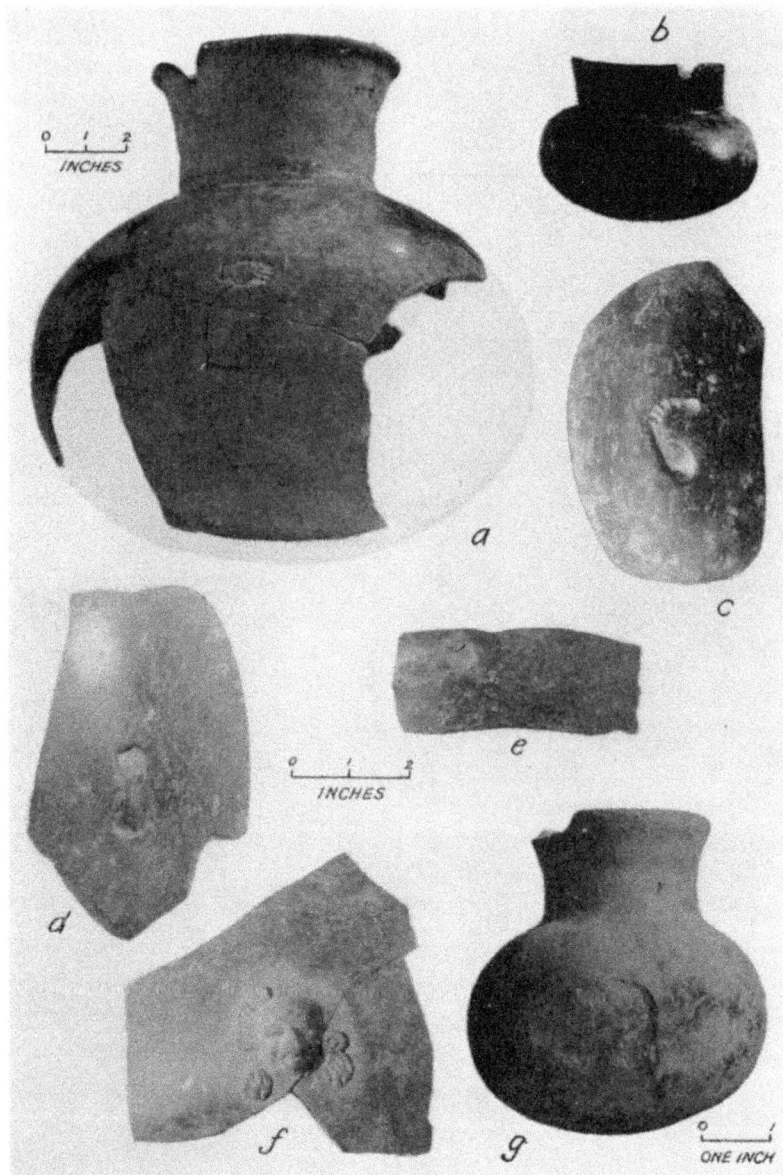

BROWN WARE OLLAS.

a–f, From trench 10; g, from burial I–3; c–e, fragments with impressed miniature footprints;
f, appliqué modeled ornament on olla-body sherd.
(Upper scale applies to a; middle scale to c, d, e, and f; lower scale to g.)

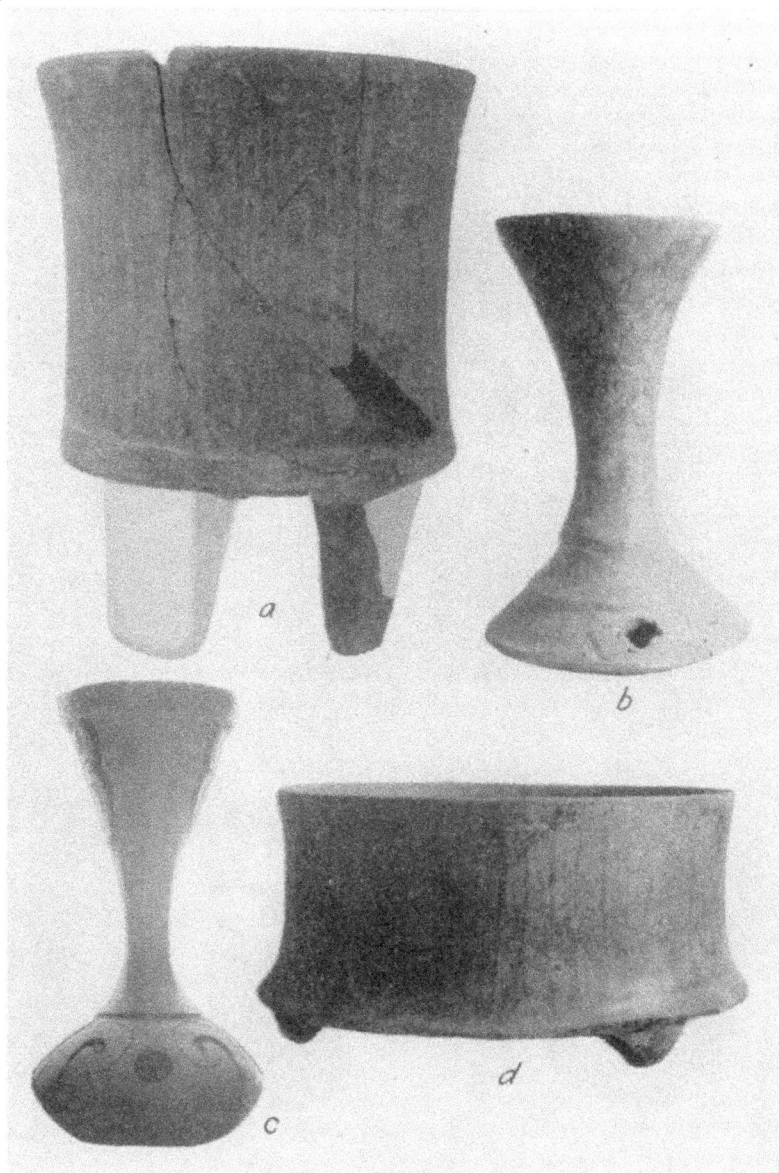

POLISHED BROWN WARE.

a, From trench 10; *b, c*, from burial I–19; *d*, from trench 34.   (Scales of figures vary.   Height of body: *b*, 7½ inches; *c*, 8¾ inches; *d*, 3½ inches.)

BLACK WARE VESSELS.

a, e, Scraped ("raspada") decoration; *f*, post-firing incised; *b–f*, miniature forms; *a*, from burial I–20; *b, c*, from burial I–5; *d–f*, from trench 30.

(Upper scale applies to *a;* lower scale to *b–f*.)

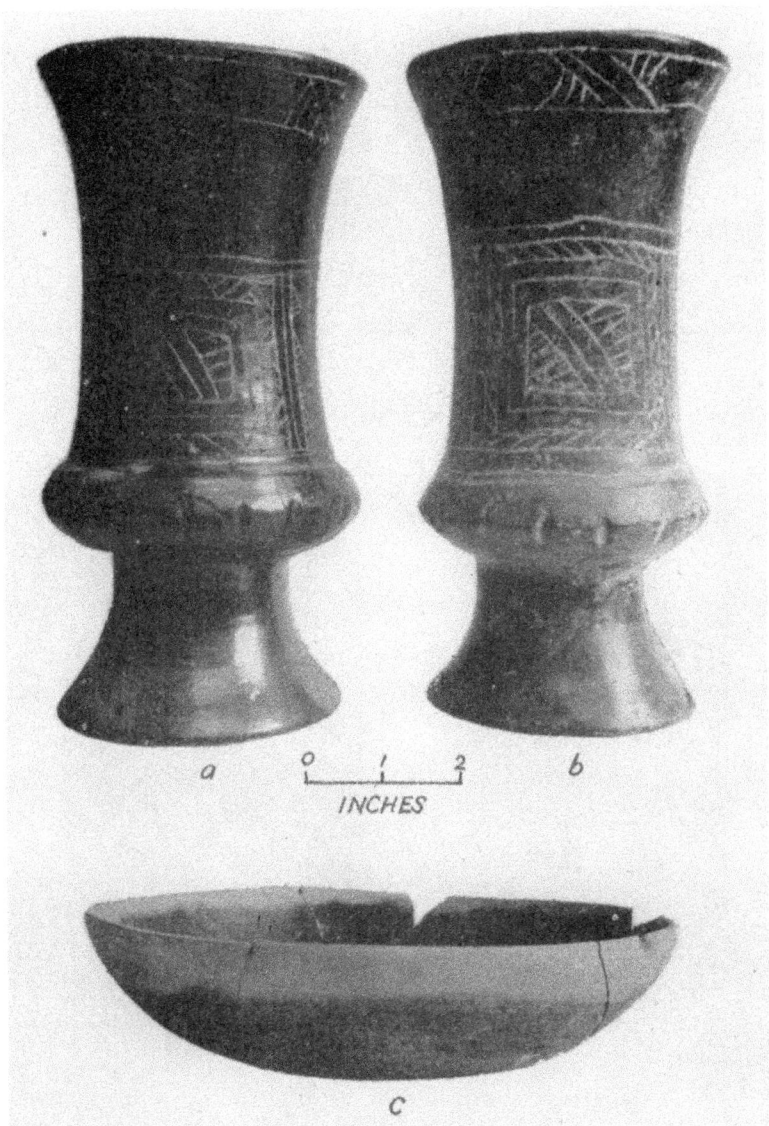

BLACK WARE VESSELS.
a, *b*, from burial I–18; *c*, White-rimmed Black ware bowl from trench 34.
(Scale applies to *a* and *b*.)

STUCCO PAINTED WARE FROM BURIAL 11–18.

The potstand *a* is to slightly larger scale than rest; actually it and *b* are very nearly of a size.

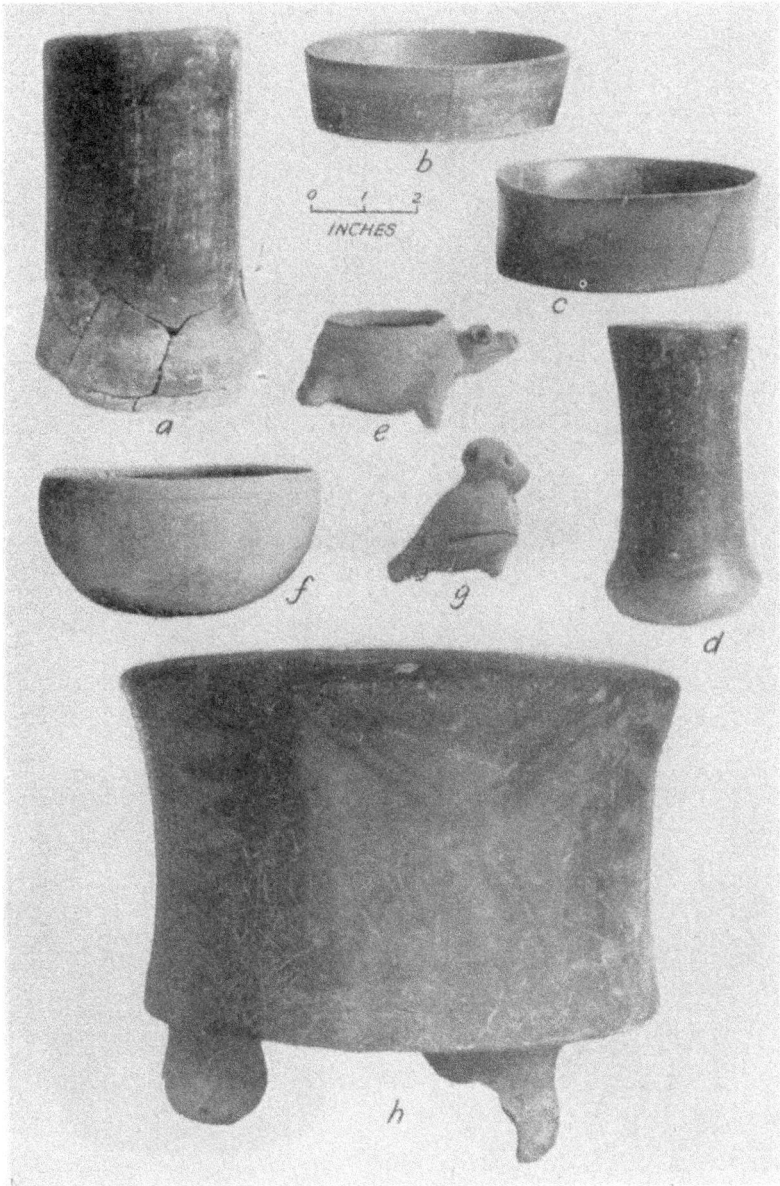

MISCELLANEOUS WARES.

a–d, Red-on-Brown; *e, f*, White; *h*, Negative Painted (Red-on-Brown).   *a, d*, From burial I–18; *b, c, h*, from trench 34; *e–g*, from burial II–3.

PLUMBATE WHISTLING JAR FROM TRENCH 15.

BOTTLES IN FORM OF TLALOCS. PURCHASE COLLECTION.

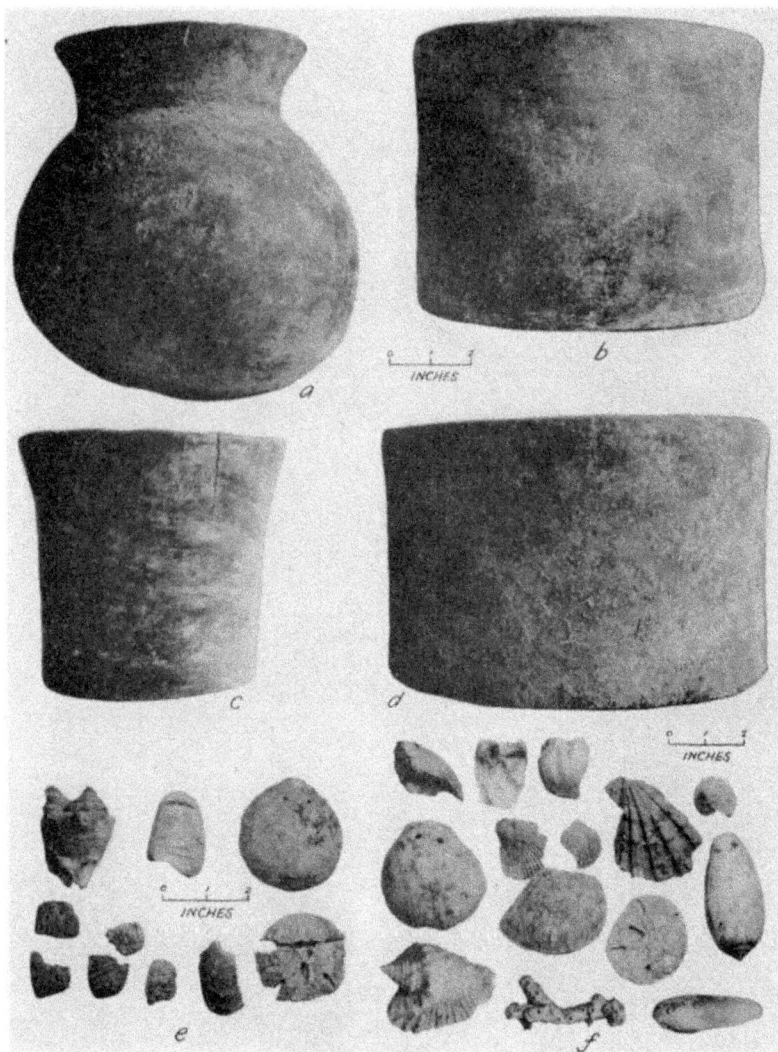

PLAIN WARE OLLAS AND JARS.

a, From trench 13; *b*, from trench 34 (see pl. 16); *c*, from trench 30 ("burial" II–18); *d*, from trench 32; *e*, contents of *b*; *f*, partial contents of several Plain ware jars from trench 34 (note parrot beak, skulls in upper left corner).

(Upper scale applies to *a–d*; middle scale to lower right group of specimens (*f*); lower scale to lower left group of specimens (*e*).)

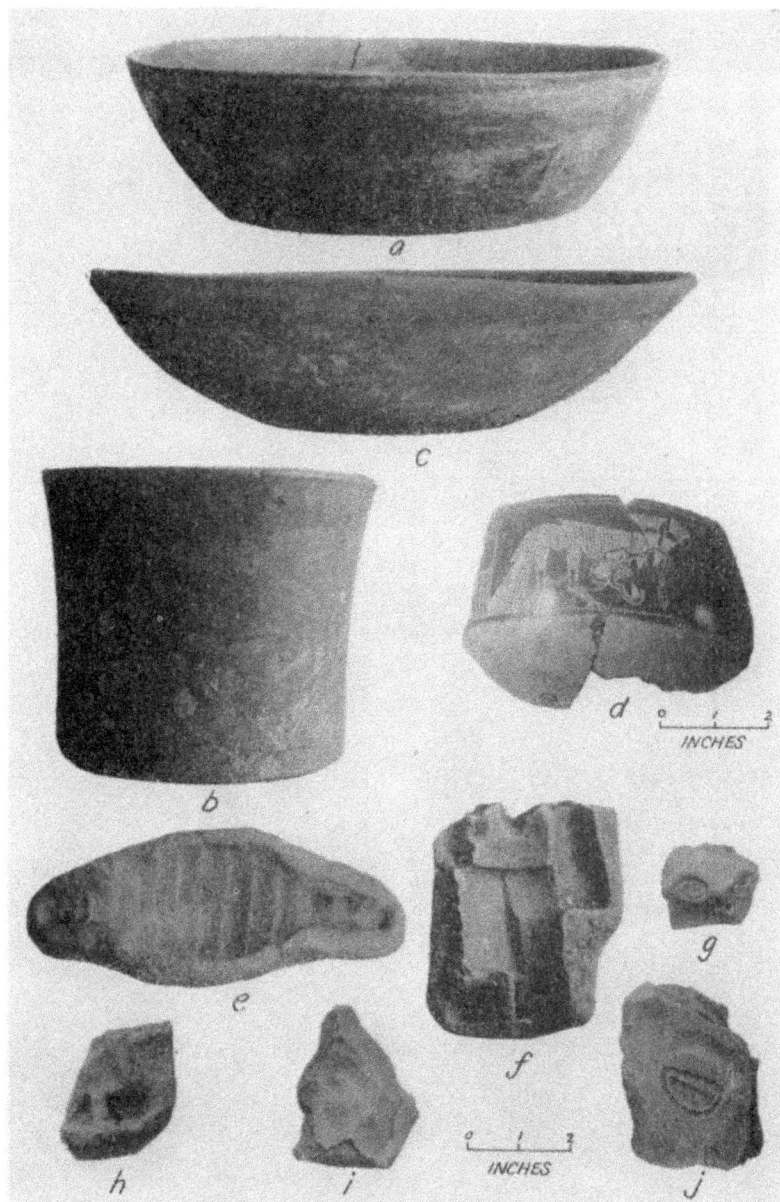

WARES AND FIGURINE MOLDS.

a, b, Red ware from trench 34; c, Coarse Red-rimmed bowl from trench 19; d, Red-on-
Orange Incised bowl fragment, with unique design, from trench 10; e–j, figurine molds,
purchase collection.

(Upper scale applies to d; lower scale to a, b, c, e–j.)

HAND-MADE PUNCTATE FIGURINES (TYPE I).

a–j, Type I–A; *k–l*, type I–D; *m–t*, type I–G; *u–cc*, type I–H. (Scale varies.)

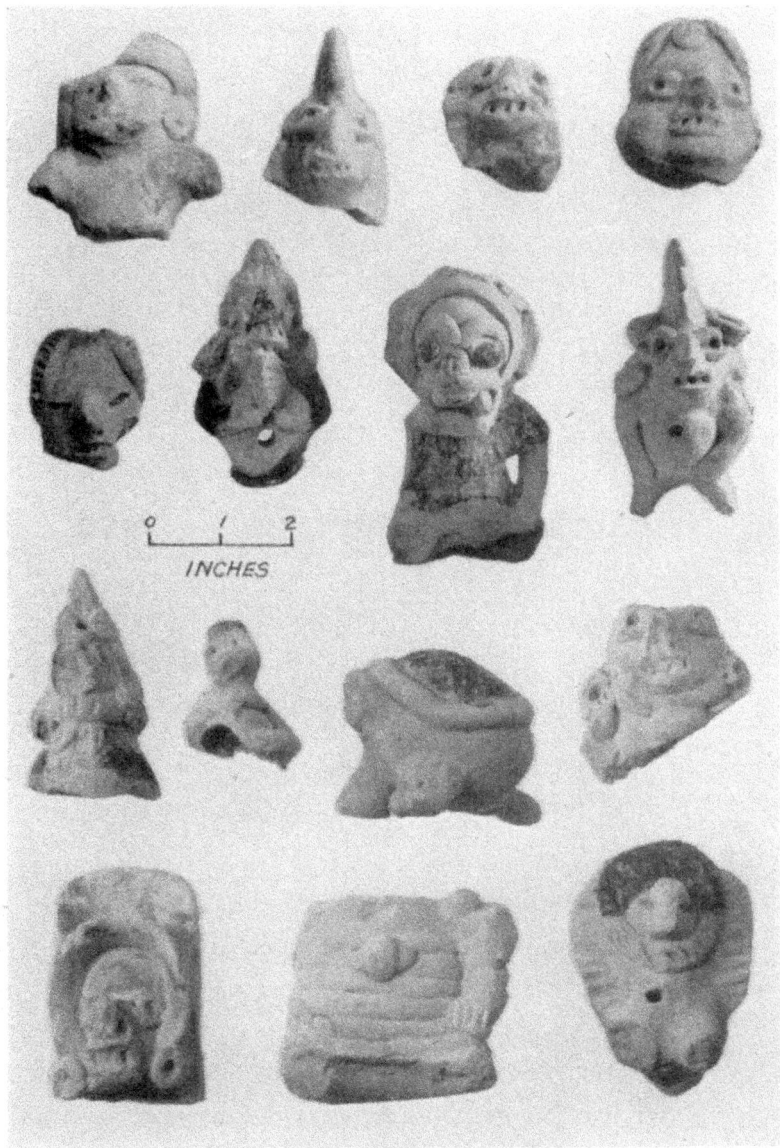

MISCELLANEOUS TYPE I FIGURINES.
Variants, animal forms, etc.

BULLETIN 141 PLATE 29

TYPE II-A FIGURINE HEADS.

TYPE II FIGURINES WITH FLAT BODIES.
(Upper scale applies to upper six figurines; lower scale to lower three figurines.)

Type II-A Figurines With Flat Bodies.

TYPE II FIGURINES WITH HOLLOW BODIES.

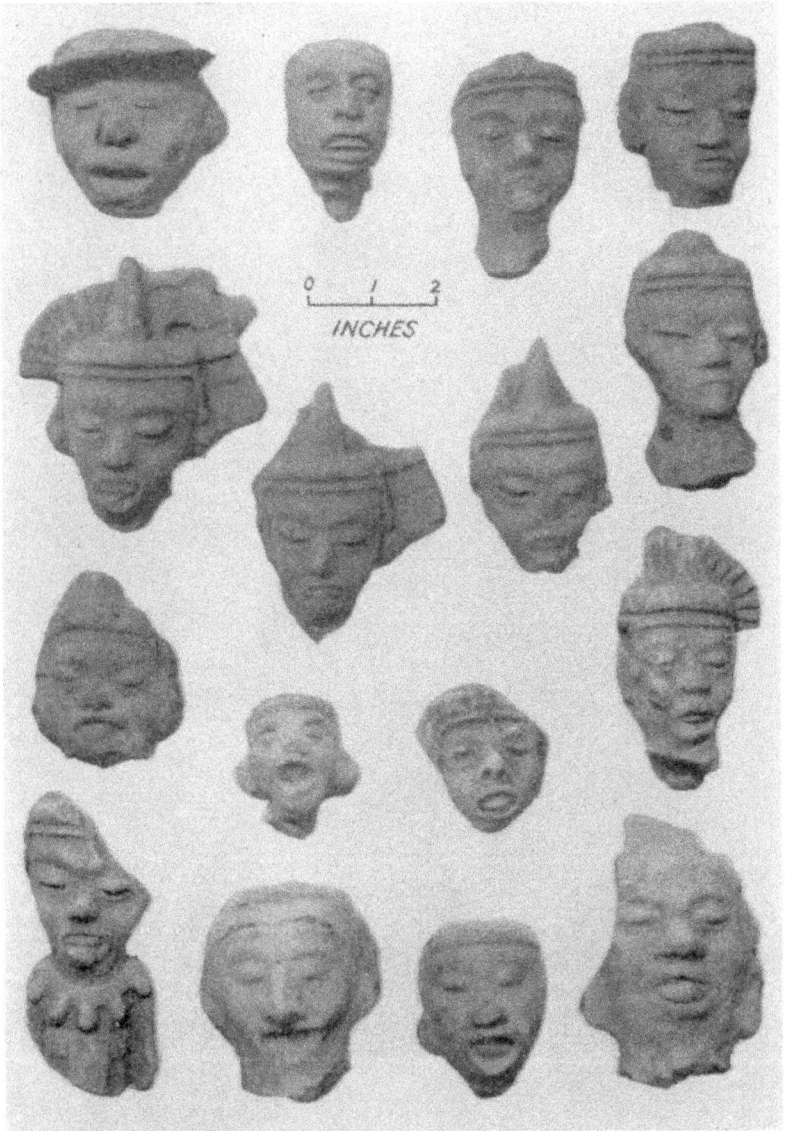

TYPE II-B FIGURINES REPRESENTING DEAD PERSONS OR XIPE.

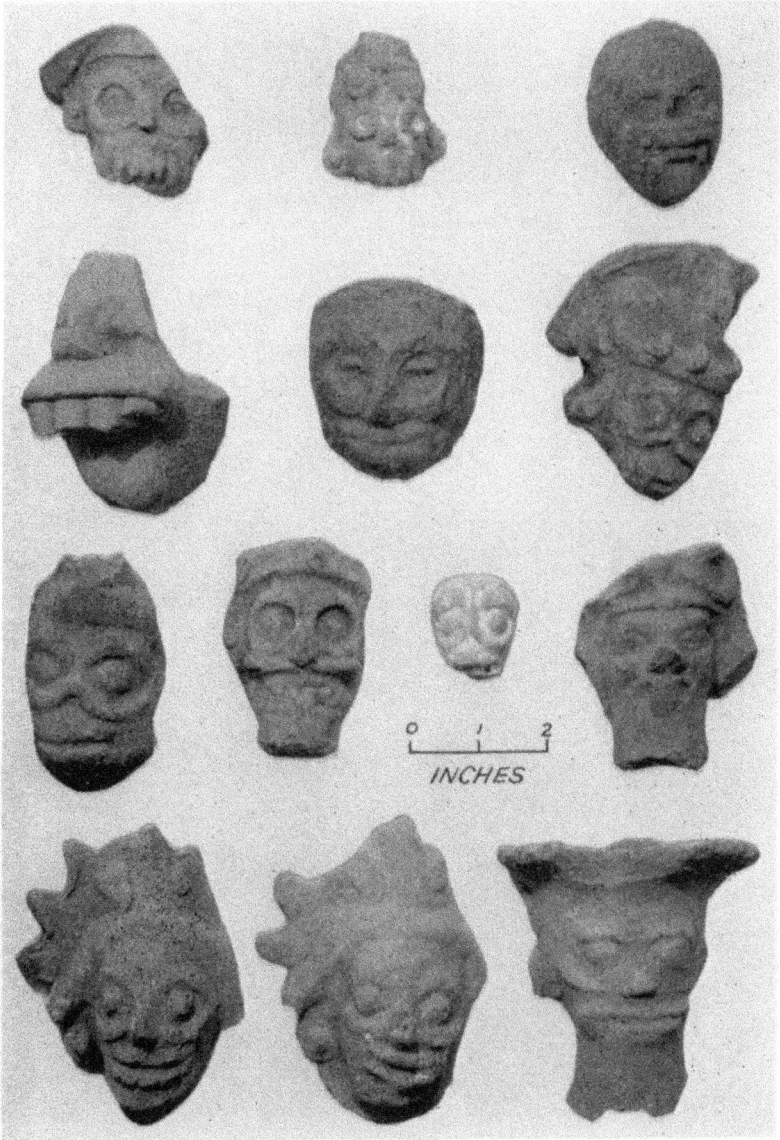

TYPE II FIGURINES, REPRESENTING TLALOCS AND DEATH'S HEADS.

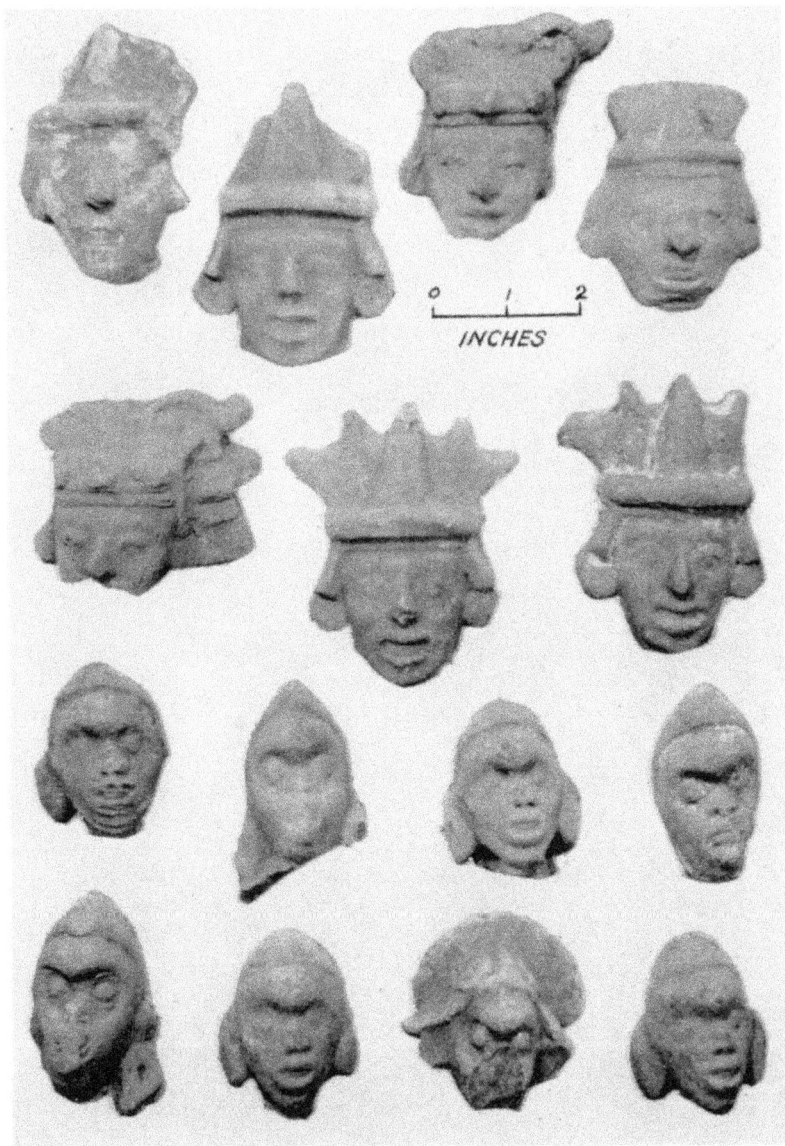

TYPE II FIGURINES
Variant Headdresses; Monkeys.

TYPE II FIGURINES, REPRESENTING ANIMALS.

VARIANT TYPE II FIGURINES.

MISCELLANEOUS TYPE II FIGURINES.

TYPE III FIGURINES

FIGURINE TYPES.

a–i, Type IV–A; *j–m*, type IV–B; *n, o*, type V.   *a, b, e, h, n, o*, from trench 10; remainder, purchase collection.

(Scale applies to *a–i*.)

FIGURINE TYPES.

a–c, Type VI; d–h, type VII (San Marcos).   b, d, g, purchase collection; remainder, from trench 10.

(Scale applies to d–h.)

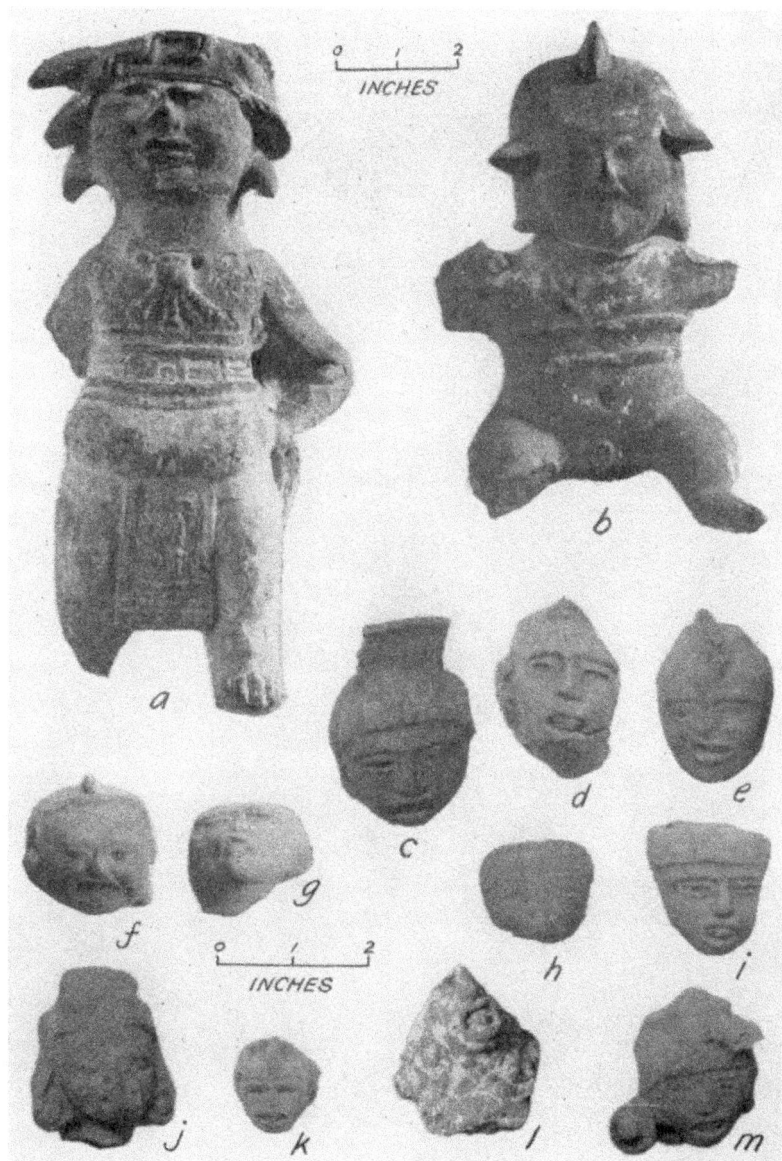

FIGURINE TYPES.

a, b, Type VIII–A; *c–m,* type VIII–B.   *a, b,* Purchase specimens from nearby Cerro del Gallo.
(Upper scale applies to *a* and *b;* lower scale to *c–m*).

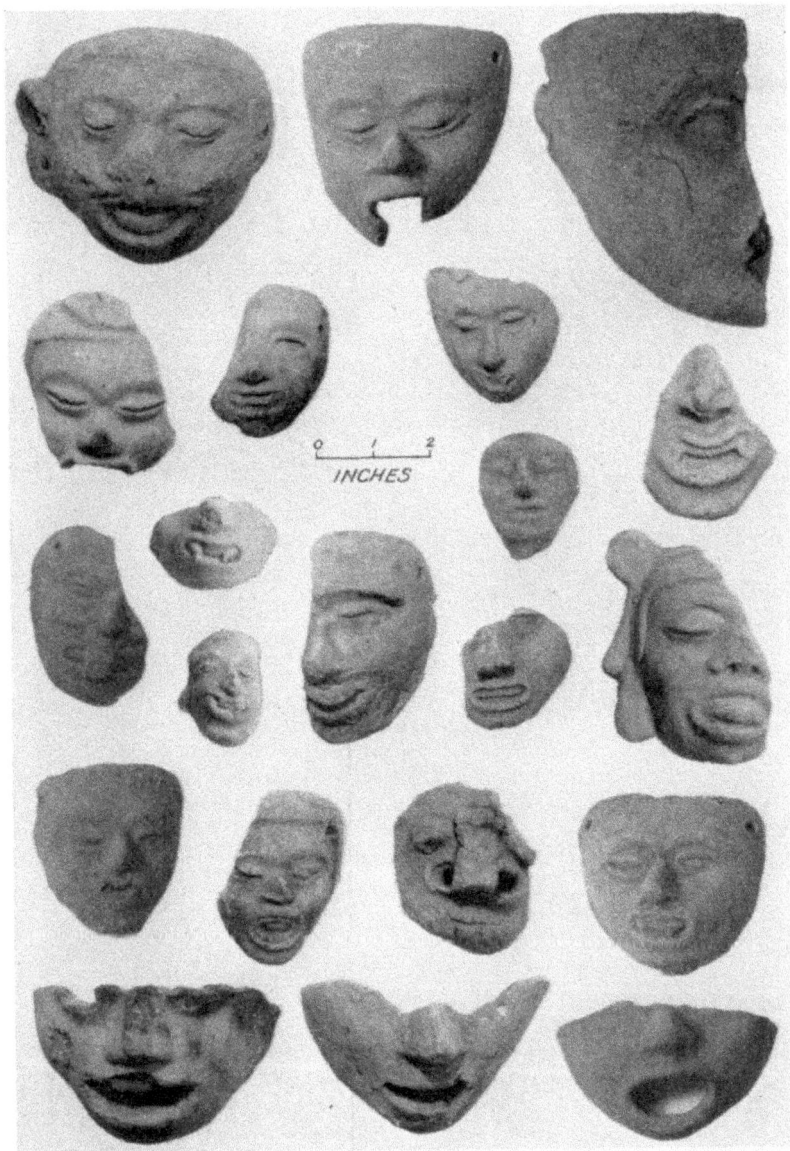

TYPE IX FIGURINES.
Masks and maskettes.

SMALL STONE OBJECTS FROM CERRO DE LAS MESAS.

MONUMENTAL WARE: IDOLS.

a–c, From purchase collection; *d*, from trench 15; *e*, from trench 34.   (*a*, 10½ inches high;
scale applies to *b*, *b'*, *c*, and *d*.)

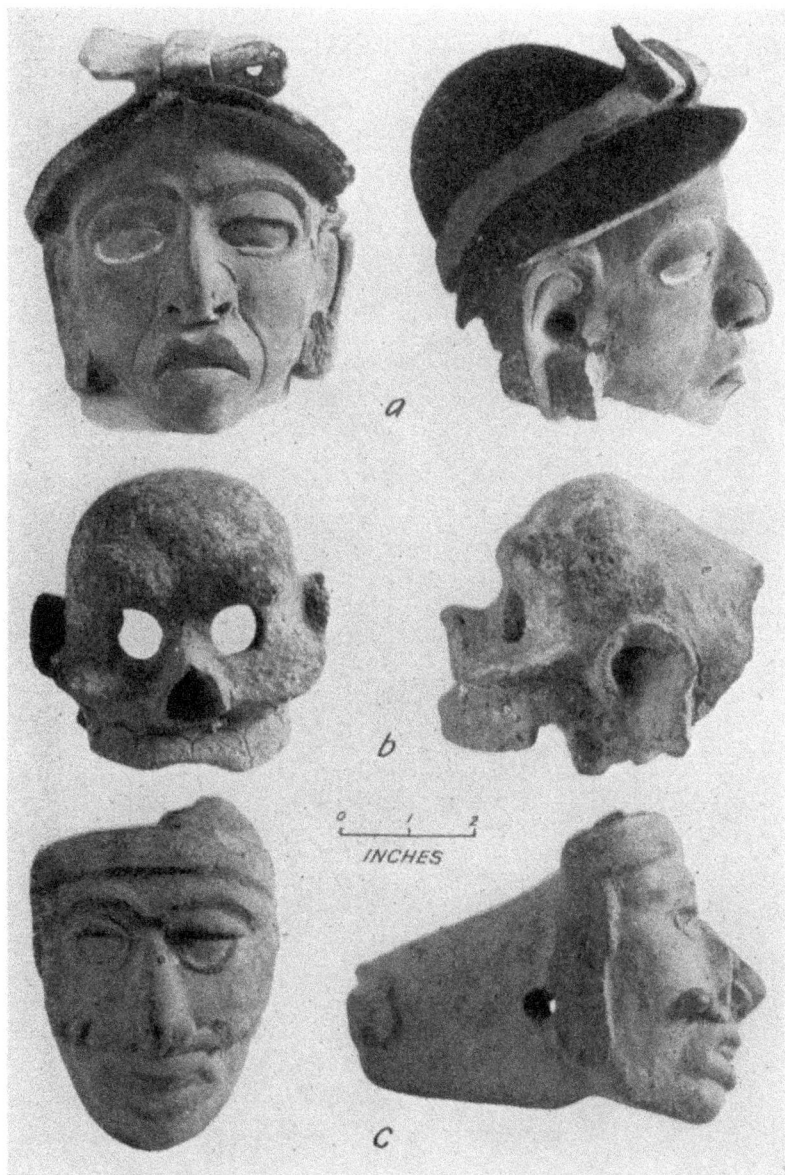

MONUMENTAL WARE: HEADS OF MEDIUM SIZE.

a, From trench 10; *b*, *c*, purchase collection. *c* is equipped with a hollow tenon, presumably for use as an architectural ornament.

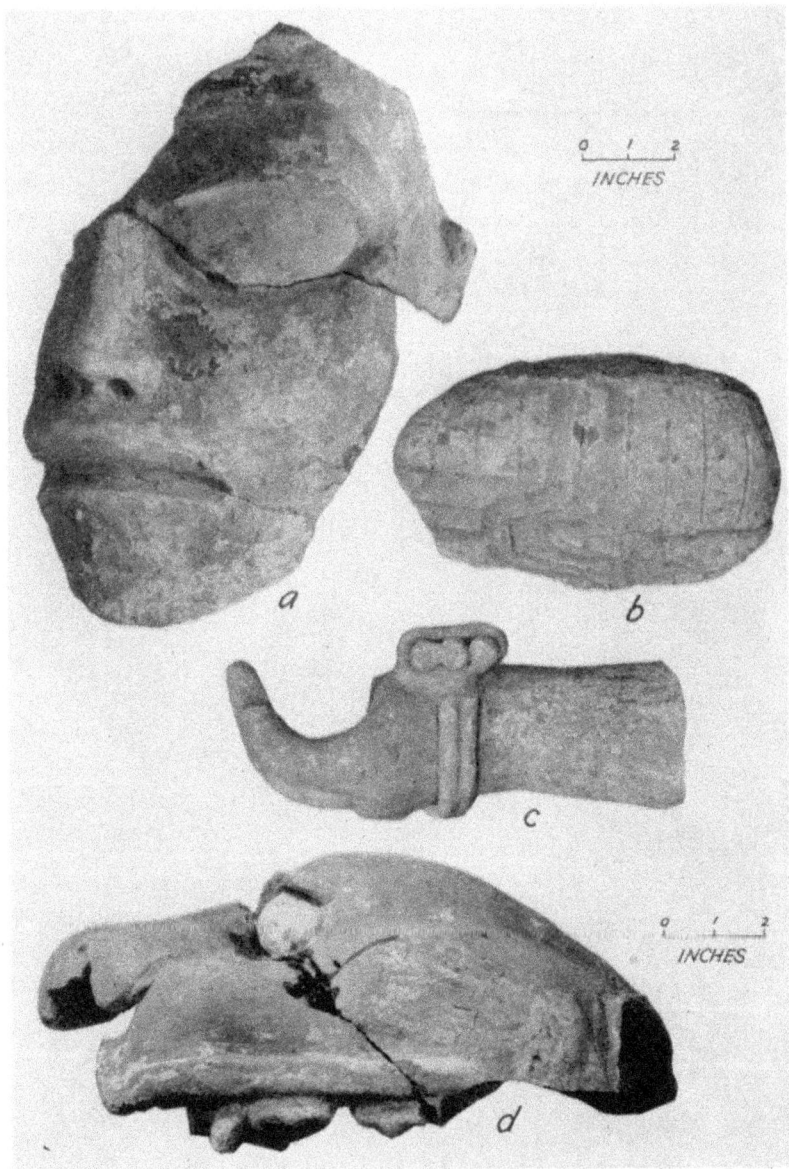

MONUMENTAL WARE: IDOLS.

a, b, c, From trench 34; *d,* from trench 31.

(Upper scale applies to *a, b, c;* lower scale to *d.*)

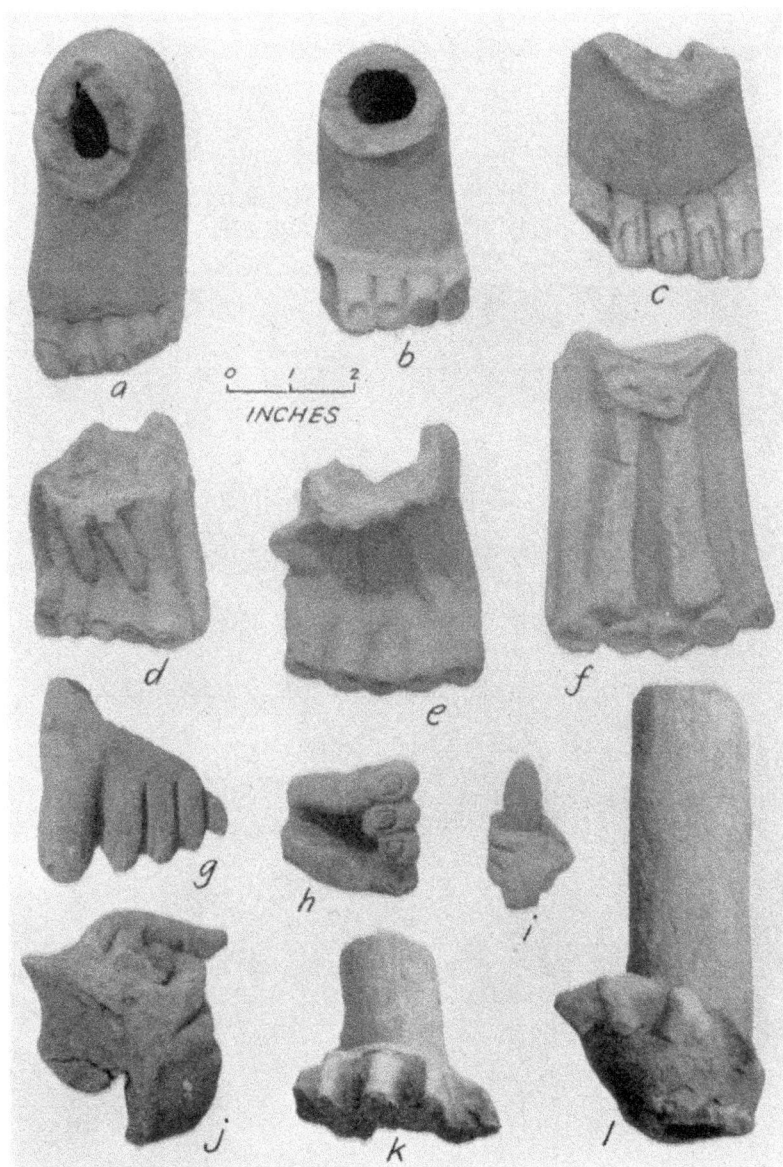

MONUMENTAL WARE: FRAGMENTS OF IDOLS.

g, From trench 10; *h–j*, from trench 34; *l*, from trench 12; remainder, from purchase collection.

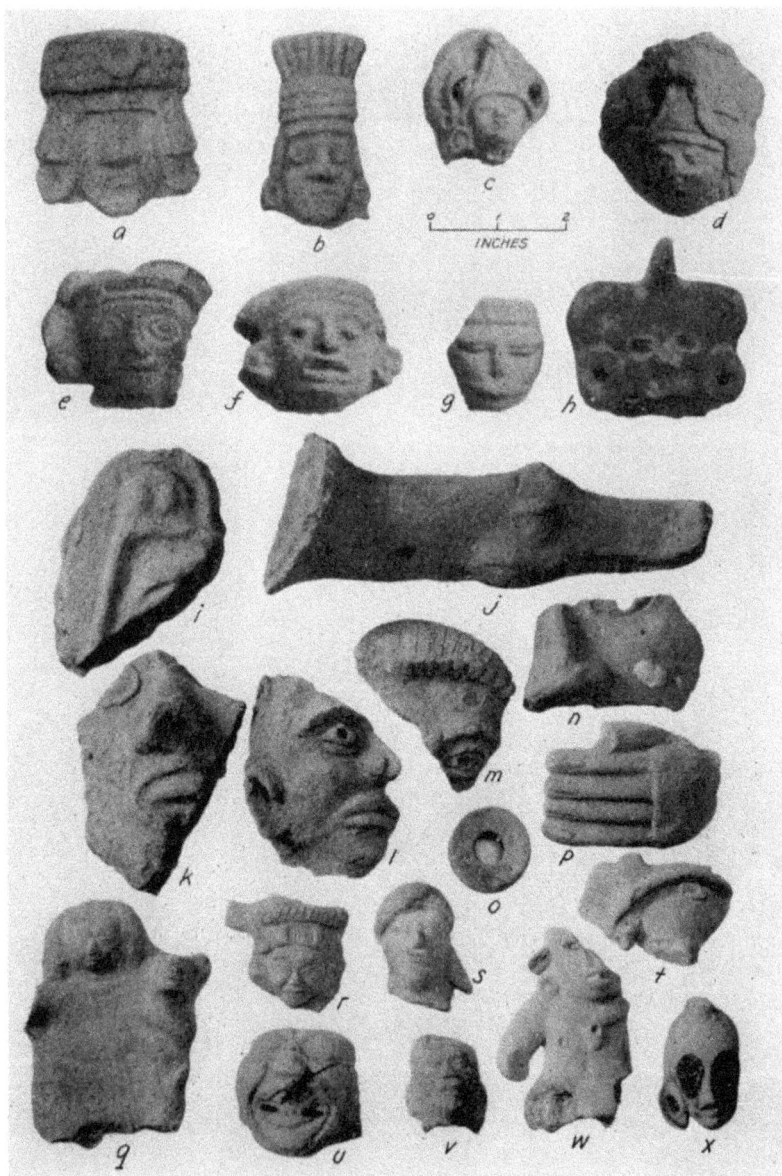

FIGURINE TYPES.

a–h, Imported and aberrant types (*a, b*, Aztec; *c, d*, Teotihuacán IV).   *i–x*. Figurine sample from trench 34.

(Scale applies to *a–h*.)

REPRESENTATIVE SAMPLES OF FIGURINES.

a, From trench 30; *b*, from trench 33.

(Scale applies to lower two rows of figurines (*b*).)

REPRESENTATIVE SAMPLES OF FIGURINES.

a, From trench 31; *b*, from trench 15.

(Upper scale applies to upper two rows of figurines (*a*); lower scale to two lower rows of figurines (*b*).)

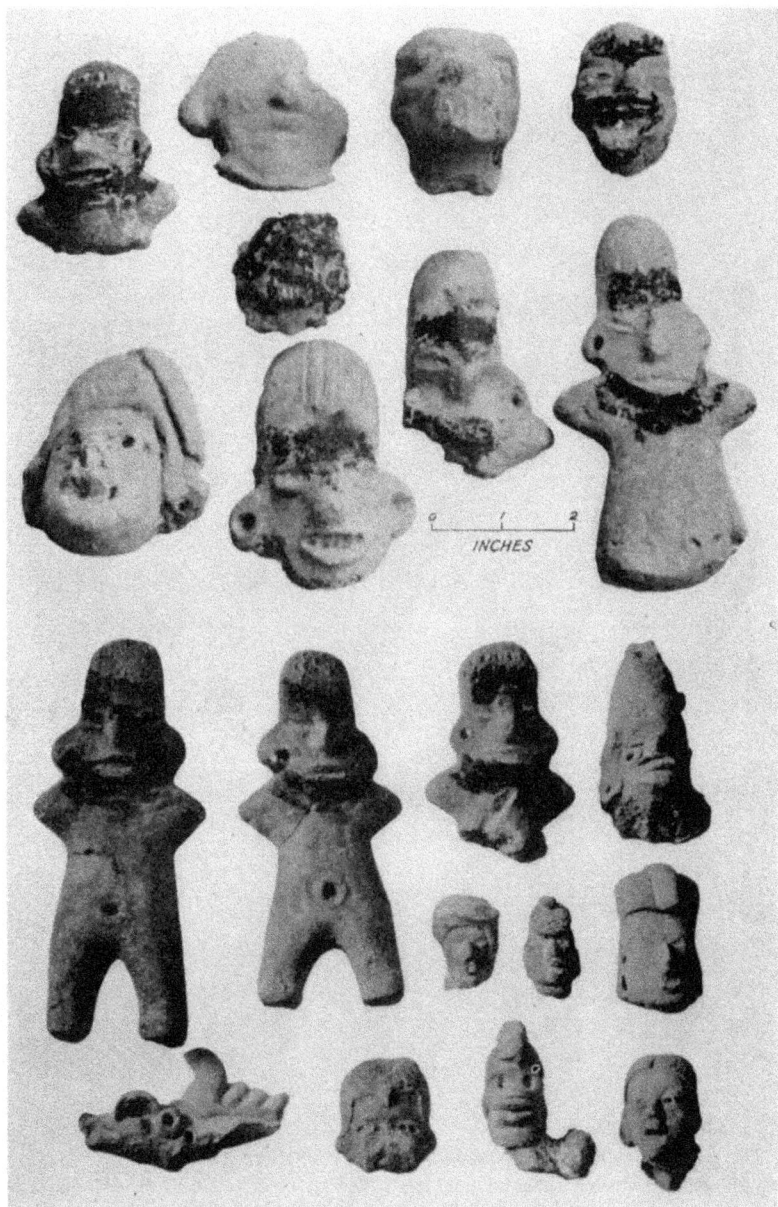

REPRESENTATIVE SAMPLES OF FIGURINES FROM TRENCH 32.
(Scale applies to upper nine figurines.)

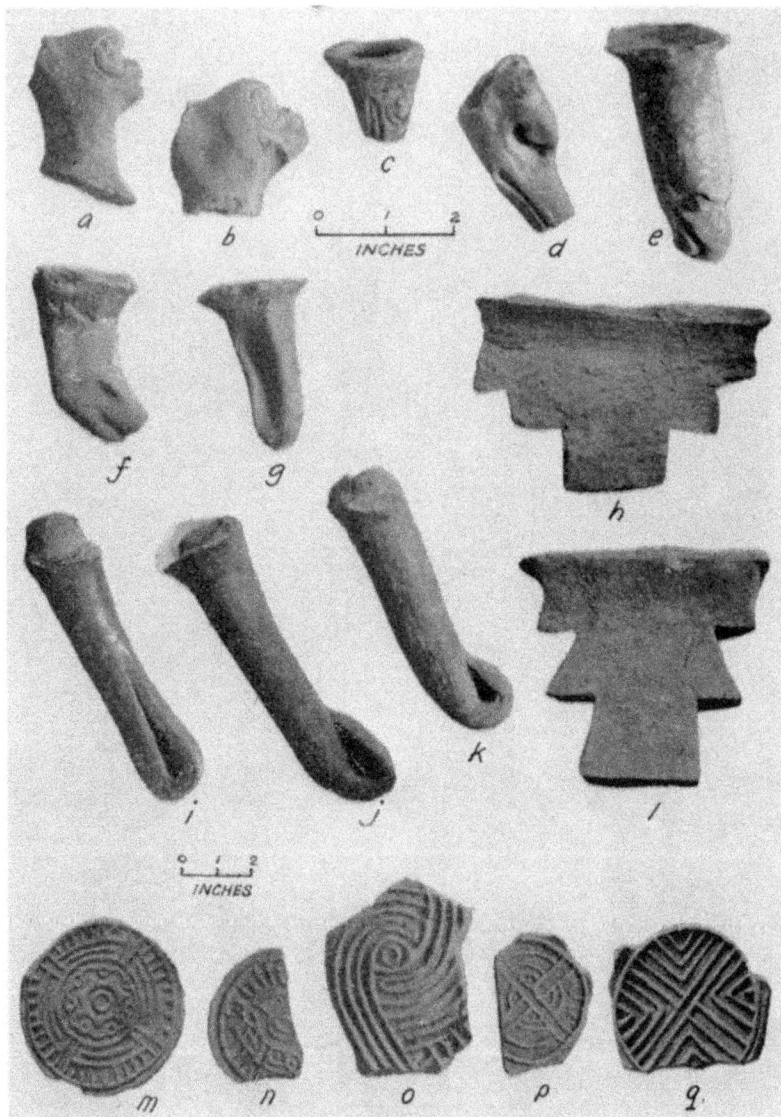

MISCELLANEOUS UPPER PHASE FEATURES.

a, *b*, Handles with zoomorphic ornament; *c–l*, various types of supports; *m–q*, bases with molded ornament (Brown Polychrome bowls).

(Upper scale applies to *a–l*; lower scale to *m–q*.)

STRATIGRAPHIC MATERIAL FROM TRENCH 42.

Only the more complete and readily identifiable pieces are shown here. *a, c, f,* Type II; *b, e,* type III; *d,* type IX; *g,* type VII–B; *h,* type IV–A or V; *i,* type I–G; *j–m, o–q, s,* type I–A (variants; *j* and *q* approach Tres Zapotes I–F, a modified form); *n,* type I–X; *r,* type I–D. *a, b,* 24– to 36–inch level; *c–f,* 36 to 48; *g,* 60 to 72; *h,* 84 to 96; *i,* 108 to 120; *j,* 132 to 134; *k–n,* 144 to 156; *o–p,* 156 to 168; *q–s,* 168 to 180.

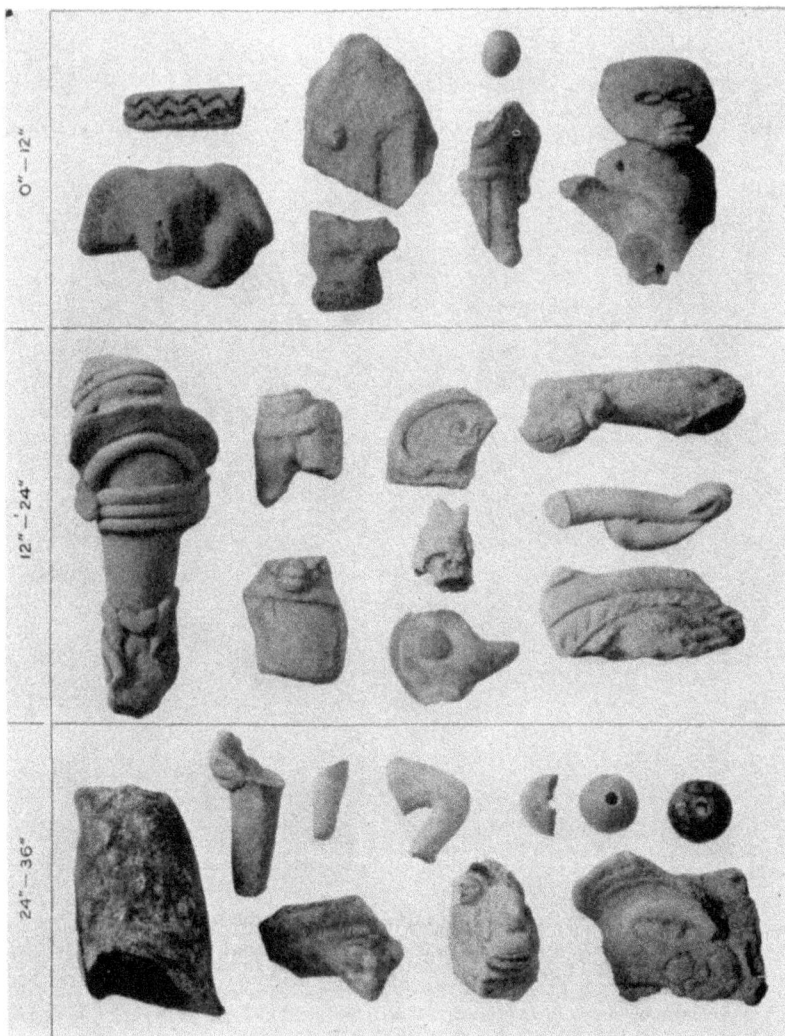

STRATIGRAPHIC MATERIAL FROM TRENCH 13.

0- to 12-inch level: (Upper row) flat seal, fragment type III figurines, clay pellet; (lower row) fragments type II figurines, fragment type VI figurine, type IV–A.

12- to 24-inch level: Leg of small type X figurine; (upper row) type VI figurine, unidentified, type IV or V; (middle row) unidentified, arm of type IV; (lower row) type VI, type IX, type I–G.

24- to 36-inch level: Vertical modeled lug; (upper row) arm and leg type IV, unidentified fragments, mold-made spindle whorls; (lower row) unique mold-made vessel support. type I–G. type VII.

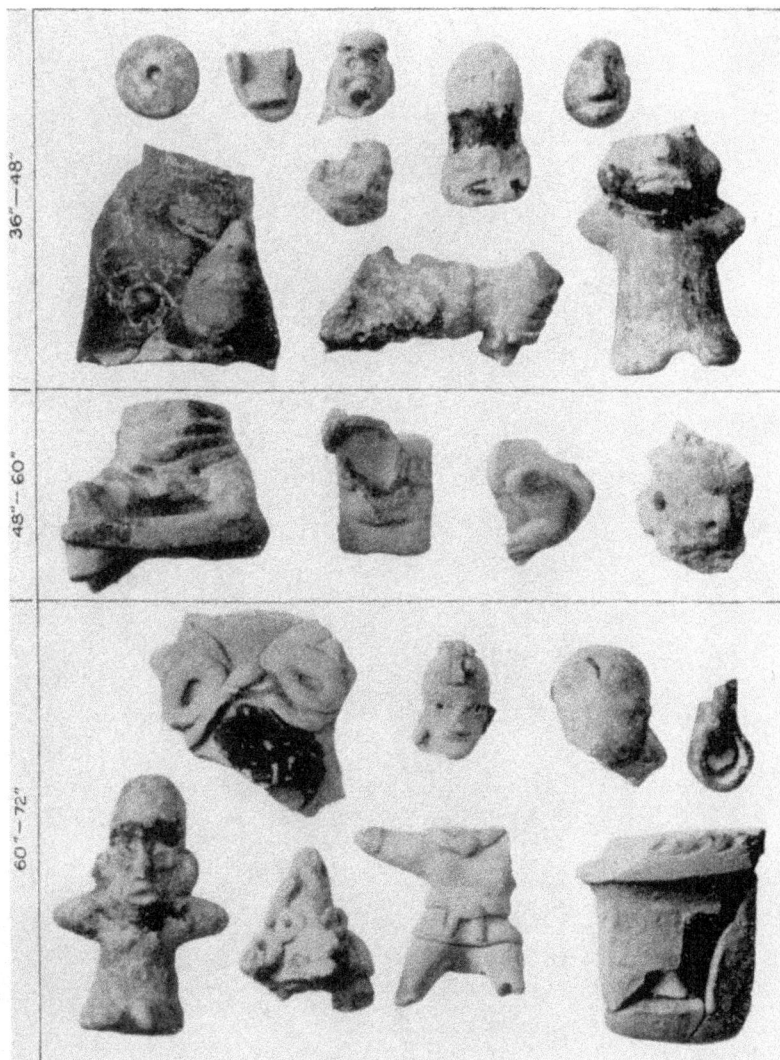

STRATIGRAPHIC MATERIAL FROM TRENCH 13.

36- to 48-inch level: (Upper row) mold-made spindle whorl, aberrant snake head, type I–X, type I–G, aberrant type; (center) type VII; (lower row) unique modeled face on olla neck suggests type I; hand possibly type X; type I–6.

48- to 60-inch level: Type IV–A, type IV or V, unidentified, type I variant.

60- to 72-inch level: (Upper row) type IV–A, type I–A variant, type I–X, double ring; (lower row) type I–G, type I–H, type IV–A body, hollow slab leg.

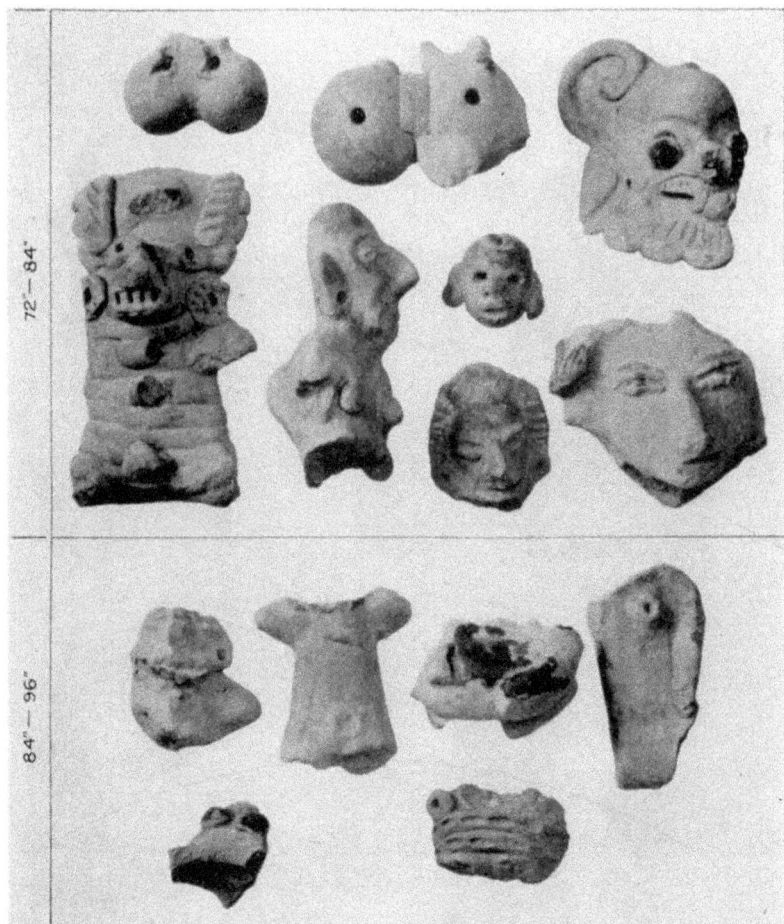

STRATIGRAPHIC MATERIAL FROM TRENCH 13.

72- to 84-inch level: (Upper row) double whistle, ocarina (unique in collections from site), type VII; (center) aberrant; (lower row) type I–H, type I aberrant, type I–H, type IV–A variant.
84- to 96-inch level: (Upper row) type I–G, type I–G, type I–X, type I indeterminate; (lower row) type IX (frog bowl), type I indeterminate.

MISCELLANEOUS STONE OBJECTS.

a, a', Marble (?) mask from Coyol (near Cerro de las Mesas); b, diorite hacha in form of jaguar head; c, stone figure associated with jade cache from trench 34; d, stone yoke from burial I–18.

www.ingramcontent.com/pod-product-compliance
Lightning Source LLC
Chambersburg PA
CBHW020442300326
41934CB00042B/370